The Screenplay Workbook

the writing *before* the writing

Jeremy Robinson
& Tom Mungovan

illustrated by
Jeremy Robinson

lone eagle™

THE SCREENPLAY WORKBOOK

WATSON-GUPTILL PUBLICATIONS, an imprint of the Crown Publishing Group,
a division of Random House, Inc., New York
www.crownpublishing.com
www.watsonguptill.com

Printed in the United States of America
10 9 8 7 6 5 4 3

Cover design by Sheri Lam and Lindsay Albert
Book design by Carla Green
ISBN: 978-1-58065-053-3

For Hilaree Robinson

and

Lisa Henderson

Without your love and support,
this book would never
have become a reality.

Contents

Acknowledgments

We would like to thank the following individuals
for their time, input and expertise:

Hilaree Robinson, for supreme editing.

Joanne Parrent, for unparalleled proposal writing advice.

Sheri Fults, Jeremy's literary manager,
for sound advice and honest critiques.

Mark Byers, Beverly Diehl and Karl Iglesias, for adding to the proposal.

Lisa Henderson, for her brilliant ideas and contributions.

The Robinson, Brodeur and Mungovan families,
for their continuing support and encouragement.

Lauren Rossini, our editor at Lone Eagle,
for making our first non-fiction experience a pleasure.

Speech bubbles: "Hi there. My name is John Q. Screenwriter. Using this book will help you avoid—" "all the screenwriting potholes I hit when I first started out." "Prepare to have fun, save time and write a blockbuster!"

Chapter 1

INTRODUCTION

For many screenwriters, the day they decide to write their first screenplay often goes something like this: while watching a movie they think to themselves, "I could do this! Heck, I could do better then this! I haven't written since high school, but if *this* film got made, my film surely would be! And then I'd be rich, rich, rich," at which point they push their fingers together in a Montgomery Burns fashion and fiendishly whisper, "Exxxcellent."

The next few steps in the budding screenwriter's development are the systematic and brutal tearing down of their misconceptions. Not only is writing a screenplay difficult—with its rigid format, page count requirements, visual writing style and realistic dialogue—screenwriting demands preparation.

Characters, layers upon layers of plot and subplot, and every emotional rise and fall the audience experiences need to be planned out in advance, like a blueprint. For years screenwriters have been creating this blueprint from scratch, spending hours compiling research and ideas scribbled out on random notebook pages. But all that is about to change.

My name is Jeremy Robinson and I am the co-author of *The Screenplay Workbook*, along with Tom Mungovan. While Tom and I are both screenwriters, we also both have backgrounds in graphic design. It was only a matter of time before Tom came to me and said, "Hey, I made this worksheet that can help us create better characters. After all, if we don't know our characters, who will?"

To which I replied, "Cool, this will make creating characters easy!"

While our dialogue may have been a little stilted, the enthusiasm was genuine. The wheels in my head began to crank (which isn't always easy to do after a day of typing in front of a glaring computer screen) and I began to have an epiphany. I asked Tom something like, "Wouldn't it be nice if we had a bunch of different worksheets that helped create and manage concepts, plots and characters?" only slightly less salesman-like sounding.

At this point, both of our collective, artistic, literary and publishing-focused minds were wrapping themselves around the inevitable creative solution: create a workbook! We began work on *The Screenplay Workbook* that day, writing introductions, instructions and creating the worksheets that I now wish existed when I started writing.

The worksheets contained in this workbook will help with the creation of characters, plots and concepts, bringing it all together into an easily understandable final product. Go through this workbook for each of your existing screenplays and find the holes you know are there, but can't see. Or simply use it to create new stories.

When you've finished all the worksheets for a single project, writing the full screenplay will be considerably easier (and better) than it would have been before.

The worksheets provided in this book are tools to be used in the creative process before you write or rewrite your screenplay. These are the first steps to creating a dynamic story filled with vivid characters. You might ask, "Why don't you write a companion how-to book to accompany *The Screenplay Workbook?* You could call it *The Screenplay Workbook Handbook!* That'd be great, right?"

> **When you've finished all the worksheets for a single project, writing the full screenplay will be considerably easier (and better) than it would have been before.**

My answer is simple. There are hundreds of how-to screenwriting books on the market, and many of them are excellent. Why would Tom or I want to write yet another "how to" screenwriting book?

This workbook is not a how-to book. It's not going to tell you how to write well. It's not going to instruct you how to write realistic dialogue or how to format a screenplay. While these are very important elements in screenwriting, they are not subjects that can be transformed into useful worksheets.

In addition to all the great screenwriting books on the market today, there are a plethora of resources available through the Internet, newsletters, magazines, managers, software, readers, published scripts, etc. With all this available to our eager fingertips, what could possibly be missing? But there is a void that exists within many a screenwriter's universe, and that is one of organization and planning. The best story can go awry if it doesn't have the strength to hold itself together.

I've been continually expanding my personal knowledge of the screenwriting craft and have explored a vast majority of available resources, but there is one thing I have never found: worksheets. This is the reason for *The Screenplay Workbook.*

Whether you're a student, a screenwriter novice, or a seasoned professional, *The Screenplay Workbook* is an invaluable tool!

Fill out the worksheets and keep them together. Keep them next to you as you write. Your completed worksheets will help you answer questions about your characters, relationships, plot and structure; they will keep you on track. The entertainment industry demands a very strict format and using the worksheets will help your screenplay, page by page.

It is our sincere hope that *The Screenplay Workbook* and its worksheets will help your writing process as much as it has helped ours.

The workbook provides you with enough worksheets for roughly five screenplays. Once you've identified the concept for your screenplay, the worksheets give you a framework to really get to know your characters and map out your masterpiece. The more forethought you put into your screenplay, the easier it will be to create something people will want to see! Now get to work on your new blockbuster—and good luck!

> Whether you're a student, a screenwriter novice, or a seasoned professional, *The Screenplay Workbook* is an invaluable tool!

—Jeremy Robinson and Tom Mungovan

John discovered why writer's block and deadlines don't mix...and why so many screenwriters are bald.

Chapter 2

CONCEPT CREATION

W ant to come up with that killer idea, but don't know where to start?

This Concept Worksheet will give you a solid foundation for you to build your own universe. The Concept Worksheet is not intended to give you a story, but it will help you decide what kind of genre, audience, elements and locations you will be interested in utilizing in your screenplay.

Concept is a basic principle and one of the first things you need to work out before you start writing. Some people say that you can create your characters first and build your story around them. This is perfectly acceptable, but very difficult, and most beginning screenwriters find that they need a concept first and their characters second.

Think about it, if you're writing something that doesn't even hold your interest, how is it going to hold a director's or a producer's? Unless you're already a pro, coming up with a concept should really be your first creative step when writing a screenplay.

Once you have a concept down, everything else will fall into place!

> **Once you have a concept down, everything else will fall into place!**

CONCEPTUALIZING: STRATEGIES TO IMPROVE YOUR CONCEPT CREATION PROCESS

Not everyone is an inexhaustible idea-generating machine, and certainly not an inexhaustible *good* idea generating machine. In fact, if you can create brilliant ideas on the spot with little or no thought, you might just be a freak of nature. If you're like most people, getting the creative juices circulating through your frontal lobe isn't as easy as just blowing you nose. If it were, we'd all discard brilliant ideas every morning like so much used tissue. Here are a few idea-inspiring techniques to aid you on your quest to be a brilliant idea nose blower.

DAYDREAM

Some may say, "Well, duh!" But chances are, even the naysayers don't really daydream. This doesn't mean, "concentrate on creating an idea." In fact, it means the exact opposite. To daydream, you must be relaxed. Let your mind drift. Move beyond the worries of the everyday and let your imagination run wild. Try asking questions like the ones below and then let yourself daydream your answers. Your imagination will soon become a powerful and flexible beast.

1. If you had the powers of Superman, what would you do?
2. If you could go back in time, where would you go?
3. If you could freeze time, what mischief would you cause?
4. If you were the main character in your favorite movie, what would you do differently?

BOOKS

Not novels (though they're great too), we're talking reference books. Most people see reference books as being boring, but all they really are is a stewpot for untold stories. But don't confine reference books to encyclopedias. There are all sorts of different reference books on all sorts of different topics. Time-Life has a number of great series. Think history. Think Space. Think paranormal. Get your hands on books about every subject that interests you. They are fodder for the mind.

COLLABORATE

Two minds are often better than one. Find another, highly creative writer, artist or filmmaker and collaborate on ideas. Better yet, get three people and start a small writer's group. Your passions will fuel each other and your individual ideas will inspire collective thinking on a grand scale. If your collaborator is a screenwriter, write a screenplay together. If your collaborator is an artist, have him or her paint or sketch scenes. If your collaborator is a filmmaker, film some scenes from your screenplay.

Being in a slump for original concepts can slow a career to a crawl, or worse, a dead stop. Don't get to the point where you run out of ideas. It's better to have hundreds of unused ideas then to have none at all. Continually create concepts, even while your writing a script. You'll find that writing comes easier and you'll be excited for your next project even before you finish the first. A steady stream of creativity is essential for a screenwriter's continued success.

JEREMY'S INSIDE SCOOP

Original thinking isn't usually encouraged in Hollywood. Most movies today are amalgams of previously successful blockbusters, rehashed for mass consumption. You'll hear screenwriters pitching their screenplays as "*The Matrix* meets *Fried Green Tomatoes*," in an effort to pique the interest of producers. If this sounds absolutely dreadful to you, you're not alone. Most screenwriters dry heave upon learning that screenplays are marketed and written this way. Here's a trick to avoid having your creativity constricted by the Hollywood python: write your film your way (concept wise, not format or structure). When you have a finished screenplay, dissect it until you can find tidbits that are reminiscent of other successful movies. If your main character is a cop with a gun—*Lethal Weapon*. If you have a fleet of space ships—*Star Wars*. Get the idea? Then, if you must present your screenplay as "*Alien* meets *Driving Miss Daisy*," you'll have it on the tip of your tongue. It won't define your screenplay, but it might you help make a sale.

EASY TO FOLLOW INSTRUCTIONS...

MOVIE GENRE

Before you can consider anything else, this is the first basic question you should ask. This is a general question that begins to narrow down possible story elements and scenarios. There are rules to each genre and your future story will have to fit the mold, or find its true genre. For example, science fiction: if the crux of your story doesn't explore or involve some kind of science, it's probably not science fiction. Circle one, two or three genres if you have to, but try to keep the number low. If your story is too broad, you may find it hard to decide on an audience.

CHARACTERS

This will determine how many characters you want to focus on. If your story is a romantic comedy, you probably want to focus on two characters; if it's science fiction, you may want an ensemble cast, like in *Star Trek* or *Star Wars*. Each choice presents its own set of challenges. If you're a first time writer, pick the set of characters that seems the least daunting, or the most exciting. You don't want to feel overwhelmed by your story before you really get started.

WHERE WILL THIS STORY TAKE PLACE?

This may not seem important at this stage but it can be. So many stories are affected by their settings. Any number of physical challenges can come into play. If your story takes place in Seattle, rain would most likely enter your story, or at least your dialogue. If you're in the Arctic: freezing temperatures, on Mars: dust storms, in Florida: hurricanes. You get the idea. Picking key locations that you are interested in writing about can sometimes generate an entire story on their own. If you've got some great locations in mind, jot them down. See what kinds of stories they inspire.

BUDGET

Okay, so, this is a boring subject that most beginning screenwriters don't think twice about. But it is important! This is the first question asked by producers, studios, directors, etc, even before they read the first page. If they have a budget of $5 million and you send them a project about Jupiter, do you really think they're going to read it? Hmm? Think about who you want to approach and this will help determine your budget. Want to write a summer sci-fi blockbuster? Then, the sky's the limit. Write whatever you can dream up. If you want to go to a small indie production company, better think twice about blowing up buildings and big budget special effects.

Be advised, the bigger your budget, no matter what the genre, the harder it may be to sell your script!

AUDIENCE

Who is going to shell out the cash to see your movie? Men or women? Grandpa or Junior? Who are you writing for? This will help determine several elements in your story. If your audience is Grandpa or Junior, you probably don't want people getting shot and blood spraying from multiple bullet wounds. Neither audience would appreciate that much. But if you want to write for men, ages 18-30, well then, break out the Uzis and AK-47s. Know your audience before you write your first page.

BASIC CONTENT OF STORY

Now that you've determined your genre, audience, characters, settings and budget, you are ready to include or remove content. Cross out content that is made impossible by your earlier choices. If you're working on a $5 million romance, you can cross out the fancy effects. When you have crossed out everything that is impossible in your story, circle the content you personally want in your story.

YOUR PERSONAL INTERESTS

This step is all about you. What have you always dreamed about writing? What places, people, or times have always intrigued you? What stories have you heard about your family that made you think, "That could make a great movie." What subjects have you always wanted to know more about? Writing a screenplay is a great excuse to research and learn (sometimes even travel).

QUICK IMPRESSION OF STORY

This is where you want to combine all the above steps into a succinct paragraph that describes your potential film. What you'll have when you're done is a basic description of your, as yet unrealized, story. Take this paragraph and expand it. Toss some characters into it and see what happens. This is your personal $E=mc^2$ before you split the literary atom.

The Screenplay Workbook
CONCEPT CREATION WORKSHEET

Screenplay/Project: _COOKIE / SINS OF THE FATHER_   Date: _5/30/10_

MOVIE GENRE

☐ Action   ☒ Suspense   ☐ Epic   ☒ Drama
☐ Romance   ☒ Thriller   ☐ Adventure   ☐ Animated
☐ Sci-Fi   ☐ Horror   ☐ Comedy   ☐ Other: _____

CHARACTERS

☐ Single Main Character   ☒ Ensemble Group - How Many? _4-6 (FAMILY)_
☐ Two Main Characters   ☐ Other: _____

WHERE WILL THIS STORY TAKE PLACE?

Location 1: _IN THE SOUTH_   Location 4: _NY_
Location 2: _WEST (CALIF)_   Location 5: _____
Location 3: _NEV_   Location 6: _____

BUDGET

☒ 0-5 million (Low Budget)   ☐ 21-200+ million (Big Budget)
☐ 5-20 million (Middle Budget)   ☐ I know exactly: $ _____

AUDIENCE

☐ Age 1-12   ☒ Age 31-40   ☒ African American   ☒ Urban
☐ Age 13-17   ☒ Age 41-50   ☐ Asian-American   ☐ Male
☒ Age 18-21   ☒ Age 51-60   ☐ Latino   ☐ Female
☒ Age 22-30   ☐ Age 61+   ☐ Other: _____

BASIC CONTENT OF STORY

☐ Romantic   ☐ Comedic   ☒ Tragedy
☐ Violent   ☐ Feel Good   ☐ CGI Special Effects
☐ Sexual   ☐ High Tech   ☐ Historic
☒ Inspirational   ☐ Supernatural   ☐ Other: _____

YOUR PERSONAL INTERESTS

VARYING TYPES DEGREES   SHED LIGHT ON HOW IMPORTANT
OF MENTAL ILLNESS   GOOD FATHERS ARE TO A
  CHILD'S DEVELOPMENT

INSPIRE FATHERS TO BE MORE
FOR THEIR CHILDREN

QUICK IMPRESSION OF STORY

HOW THE ACTIONS OR LACK OF OF AN ABUSIVE FATHER SHAPE THE LIVES
OF HIS THREE DAUGHTERS

The Screenplay Workbook — CONCEPT CREATION WORKSHEET

Screenplay/Project: _____   Date: _____

MOVIE GENRE

☐ Action   ☐ Suspense   ☐ Epic   ☐ Drama

☐ Romance   ☐ Thriller   ☐ Adventure   ☐ Animated

☐ Sci-Fi   ☐ Horror   ☐ Comedy   ☐ Other: _____

CHARACTERS

☐ Single Main Character   ☐ Ensemble Group - How Many?_____

☐ Two Main Characters   ☐ Other: _____

WHERE WILL THIS STORY TAKE PLACE?

Location 1: _____ Location 4: _____

Location 2: _____ Location 5: _____

Location 3: _____ Location 6: _____

BUDGET

☐ 0-5 million (Low Budget)   ☐ 21-200+ million (Big Budget)

☐ 5-20 million (Middle Budget)   ☐ I know exactly: $ _____

AUDIENCE

☐ Age 1-12   ☐ Age 31-40   ☐ African American   ☐ Urban

☐ Age 13-17   ☐ Age 41-50   ☐ Asian-American   ☐ Male

☐ Age 18-21   ☐ Age 51-60   ☐ Latino   ☐ Female

☐ Age 22-30   ☐ Age 61+   ☐ Other: _____

BASIC CONTENT OF STORY

☐ Romantic   ☐ Comedic   ☐ Tragedy

☐ Violent   ☐ Feel Good   ☐ CGI Special Effects

☐ Sexual   ☐ High Tech   ☐ Historic

☐ Inspirational   ☐ Supernatural   ☐ Other: _____

YOUR PERSONAL INTERESTS

_____ _____ _____

_____ _____ _____

_____ _____ _____

QUICK IMPRESSION OF STORY

_____

_____

_____

_____

The Screenplay Workbook

CONCEPT CREATION WORKSHEET

Screenplay/Project: _____   Date: _____

MOVIE GENRE

☐ Action   ☐ Suspense   ☐ Epic   ☐ Drama

☐ Romance   ☐ Thriller   ☐ Adventure   ☐ Animated

☐ Sci-Fi   ☐ Horror   ☐ Comedy   ☐ Other: _____

CHARACTERS

☐ Single Main Character   ☐ Ensemble Group - How Many? _____

☐ Two Main Characters   ☐ Other: _____

WHERE WILL THIS STORY TAKE PLACE?

Location 1: _____   Location 4: _____

Location 2: _____   Location 5: _____

Location 3: _____   Location 6: _____

BUDGET

☐ 0-5 million (Low Budget)   ☐ 21-200+ million (Big Budget)

☐ 5-20 million (Middle Budget)   ☐ I know exactly: $ _____

AUDIENCE

☐ Age 1-12   ☐ Age 31-40   ☐ African American   ☐ Urban

☐ Age 13-17   ☐ Age 41-50   ☐ Asian-American   ☐ Male

☐ Age 18-21   ☐ Age 51-60   ☐ Latino   ☐ Female

☐ Age 22-30   ☐ Age 61+   ☐ Other: _____

BASIC CONTENT OF STORY

☐ Romantic   ☐ Comedic   ☐ Tragedy

☐ Violent   ☐ Feel Good   ☐ CGI Special Effects

☐ Sexual   ☐ High Tech   ☐ Historic

☐ Inspirational   ☐ Supernatural   ☐ Other: _____

YOUR PERSONAL INTERESTS

_____ _____ _____

_____ _____ _____

_____ _____ _____

QUICK IMPRESSION OF STORY

_____

_____

_____

_____

The Screenplay Workbook

CONCEPT CREATION WORKSHEET

Screenplay/Project: _____ Date: _____

MOVIE GENRE

☐ Action   ☐ Suspense   ☐ Epic   ☐ Drama

☐ Romance   ☐ Thriller   ☐ Adventure   ☐ Animated

☐ Sci-Fi   ☐ Horror   ☐ Comedy   ☐ Other: _____

CHARACTERS

☐ Single Main Character   ☐ Ensemble Group - How Many? _____

☐ Two Main Characters   ☐ Other: _____

WHERE WILL THIS STORY TAKE PLACE?

Location 1: _____   Location 4: _____

Location 2: _____   Location 5: _____

Location 3: _____   Location 6: _____

BUDGET

☐ 0-5 million (Low Budget)   ☐ 21-200+ million (Big Budget)

☐ 5-20 million (Middle Budget)   ☐ I know exactly: $ _____

AUDIENCE

☐ Age 1-12   ☐ Age 31-40   ☐ African American   ☐ Urban

☐ Age 13-17   ☐ Age 41-50   ☐ Asian-American   ☐ Male

☐ Age 18-21   ☐ Age 51-60   ☐ Latino   ☐ Female

☐ Age 22-30   ☐ Age 61+   ☐ Other: _____

BASIC CONTENT OF STORY

☐ Romantic   ☐ Comedic   ☐ Tragedy

☐ Violent   ☐ Feel Good   ☐ CGI Special Effects

☐ Sexual   ☐ High Tech   ☐ Historic

☐ Inspirational   ☐ Supernatural   ☐ Other: _____

YOUR PERSONAL INTERESTS

_____   _____   _____

_____   _____   _____

_____   _____   _____

QUICK IMPRESSION OF STORY

_____

_____

_____

The Screenplay Workbook
CONCEPT CREATION WORKSHEET

Screenplay/Project: _____ Date: _____

MOVIE GENRE

☐ Action   ☐ Suspense   ☐ Epic   ☐ Drama
☐ Romance   ☐ Thriller   ☐ Adventure   ☐ Animated
☐ Sci-Fi   ☐ Horror   ☐ Comedy   ☐ Other: _____

CHARACTERS

☐ Single Main Character   ☐ Ensemble Group - How Many? _____
☐ Two Main Characters   ☐ Other: _____

WHERE WILL THIS STORY TAKE PLACE?

Location 1: _____   Location 4: _____

Location 2: _____   Location 5: _____

Location 3: _____   Location 6: _____

BUDGET

☐ 0-5 million (Low Budget)   ☐ 21-200+ million (Big Budget)
☐ 5-20 million (Middle Budget)   ☐ I know exactly: $ _____

AUDIENCE

☐ Age 1-12   ☐ Age 31-40   ☐ African American   ☐ Urban
☐ Age 13-17   ☐ Age 41-50   ☐ Asian-American   ☐ Male
☐ Age 18-21   ☐ Age 51-60   ☐ Latino   ☐ Female
☐ Age 22-30   ☐ Age 61+   ☐ Other: _____

BASIC CONTENT OF STORY

☐ Romantic   ☐ Comedic   ☐ Tragedy
☐ Violent   ☐ Feel Good   ☐ CGI Special Effects
☐ Sexual   ☐ High Tech   ☐ Historic
☐ Inspirational   ☐ Supernatural   ☐ Other: _____

YOUR PERSONAL INTERESTS

_____   _____   _____

_____   _____   _____

_____   _____   _____

QUICK IMPRESSION OF STORY

_____

_____

_____

_____

Screenplay/Project: _____   Date: _____

MOVIE GENRE

☐ Action   ☐ Suspense   ☐ Epic   ☐ Drama
☐ Romance   ☐ Thriller   ☐ Adventure   ☐ Animated
☐ Sci-Fi   ☐ Horror   ☐ Comedy   ☐ Other: _____

CHARACTERS

☐ Single Main Character   ☐ Ensemble Group - How Many? _____
☐ Two Main Characters   ☐ Other: _____

WHERE WILL THIS STORY TAKE PLACE?

Location 1: _____   Location 4: _____

Location 2: _____   Location 5: _____

Location 3: _____   Location 6: _____

BUDGET

☐ 0-5 million (Low Budget)   ☐ 21-200+ million (Big Budget)
☐ 5-20 million (Middle Budget)   ☐ I know exactly: $ _____

AUDIENCE

☐ Age 1-12   ☐ Age 31-40   ☐ African American   ☐ Urban
☐ Age 13-17   ☐ Age 41-50   ☐ Asian-American   ☐ Male
☐ Age 18-21   ☐ Age 51-60   ☐ Latino   ☐ Female
☐ Age 22-30   ☐ Age 61+   ☐ Other: _____

BASIC CONTENT OF STORY

☐ Romantic   ☐ Comedic   ☐ Tragedy
☐ Violent   ☐ Feel Good   ☐ CGI Special Effects
☐ Sexual   ☐ High Tech   ☐ Historic
☐ Inspirational   ☐ Supernatural   ☐ Other: _____

YOUR PERSONAL INTERESTS

_____   _____   _____

_____   _____   _____

_____   _____   _____

QUICK IMPRESSION OF STORY

_____

_____

_____

John learns the importance of not having the vegetarian on page ten order a steak on page fourteen.

Chapter 3

CHARACTER DEVELOPMENT

The most important part of a screenplay is concept, right? You have something completely new, an eye-popping idea that is sure to stun the world. That's all you need. Just stick some characters in and you'll be golden, right? Wrong!

While concept usually comes first and is often the element that grabs an audience's initial attention, it is not the most important part of a screenplay. It's hard for most of us to admit, but it's true. You may have a killer concept, but if you use flat, boring, stereotypical characters, it's still going to fall apart. No one is going to care about your great concept if they can't identify with your characters.

How does the audience identify with your character? How do you go about making that happen? If you start writing without first developing your characters, which many novice writers do, your characters will be full of inconsistencies that an audience will pick up on right away. Know your characters inside and out, past, present and future. Know their passions, weaknesses and favorite colors; every aspect of their lives should be on the forefront of your brain.

Your characters should be real people, even if they are super human. They need to feel, eat, breathe, love and hate. They should have hobbies, habits, speech patterns and physical mannerisms. They need to be consistently inconsistent—just like every other person on the planet.

More importantly, when you sit down to write your screenplay, if you know your characters, the time it takes you to write your opus will shrink dramatically. How your character speaks, acts and reacts to situations can be easily applied and understood. You won't have to try to patch together a character on the fly, and the preparation you've put into your screenplay will pay off.

A great concept is what we remember before we see the movie.
A great character is what we remember after we see the movie.

Try to keep this in mind when you are developing your characters. Make your characters unforgettable and your amazing concept will stand the test of time.

CHOOSING A NAME

What's in a name? How important is your character's name? Does it really matter what you name a character? Aren't characters defined by what they do and say?

Names are as important to your story as they are to parents naming their children. Names can define who a character is, isn't and wants to become. Imagine if you had an evil villain named Petey. Not too sinister sounding. Unless you're writing a comedy, Petey is doomed to be a pathetic villain, solely by his name, no matter how many people he kills, cities he destroys or civilizations he wipes out. You want your name to help clarify what your character is all about. Here are several strategies for discovering the perfect name for your character:

THEME

Let's say that a major theme in your story is betrayal. What's the first name that comes to mind when you think of betrayal? How about Judas—the most famous betrayer of all time? But using the name Judas is a little too obvious. Your audience will not only suspect Judas is a betrayer; they'll know it. You could be subtler by using variations of the name—Jude, Judd, Judy, Judith, Judson and Judah are good replacements. If your screenplay had environmental overtones and you wanted your main character to reflect that theme, you could name her Sarah Green. The last name Green automatically tells the audience she's on the side of nature. And if your audience is really on the ball they'll know the name Sarah means Princess. The name Sarah Green could be translated to mean: Princess of the Environment, which brings us to our next naming technique...

MEANING

Every name has a meaning. Utilizing this fact can be a very effective way to name your characters. Granted, your audience isn't going to know the definition for every name you use, but their sub-conscious may. This technique is less for the audience and more for the writer. Knowing the meaning for a particular name can help your brain focus on the character; what is at their core, where their destiny lies. (An excellent resource for finding names based on meaning is www.baby-names.com.)

SOUNDS LIKE

Names can sound like emotions, places, actions, etc. Giving a character a name that rings of something the audience recognizes can identify the character without a long explanation. Let's say you have a character in your story whose name is Avery. It's not much of a stretch to see that Avery's outstanding quality might be bravery. Here's another example: The name Hilary sounds like hilarious, right? Your audience is going to assume that the character of Hilary is a happy person based on what they read into the name. It's also not surprising that the definition for the name Hilary is cheerful.

THE OBVIOUS

This is technique is most often used in gangster movies and comic books. A woman with red hair might be named Red. A man with a square head could be named The Cube. Take a look at Spiderman's Arch nemesis, Dr. Octopus, aptly named as he has two arms, two legs and four extra, adamantium (a metal) appendages for a total of eight limbs—like an octopus. But it doesn't stop there. Look at Dr. Octopus's real name (his non-super villain name) Dr. Octo Octavius. That pretty much screams, "This guy has eight legs!" Using this technique works in some genres, but not all. Avoid naming hairy men in your drama Harry. It won't go over well. Genres where obvious naming works best are comic book, comedy and gangster films.

TOOLS OF THE TRADE

This strategy is great and may or may not incorporate the previous techniques. It's very simple: Get a thesaurus! Now think of words that describe who your character is, what he believes, what his goals are. Look that word up in the thesaurus and use the antonyms you discover to create a name. You'll find great material for "sounds like" names. You'll dig up mythological names. You'll uncover new words, which could be unique names in themselves. Using a thesaurus will open doors you never considered. (If you don't already have a thesaurus you should be ashamed. You're a writer! Go get one!) If you prefer the modern method of doing just about everything, go to: www.dictionary.com, an online dictionary and thesaurus containing (what feels like) every word imaginable.

JEREMY'S INSIDE SCOOP

Format, format, format. It's amazing how many screenwriters ignore this simple, yet infinitely important rule of screenwriting. I understand that most budding screenwriters are broke, but in the long run, picking up a copy of some screenwriting software is worth the cash. I recommend, as do most professional screenwriters, Final Draft. Save your pennies, put it on your birthday or Christmas wish list if you have to, but get a copy. Why is format important? Readers, agents and producers have become script-siphoning machines. They weed through mounds of scripts everyday and can smell an amateur miles away. Using odd formatting broadcasts that you haven't even done the very basic research to find out how to format a screenplay (which is infinitely easier then actually writing a screenplay). Improper formatting gives the reader an excuse to rip out each page of your screenplay and practice his basketball shot with the trash barrel.

EASY TO FOLLOW INSTRUCTIONS...

The character creation worksheet is basically self-explanatory.

We have provided a series of questions to answer regarding your characters. You should have an answer for every one of these questions for every major character. Keep in mind that this worksheet is merely a starting point for getting to know your characters. Come up with your own questions to ask your characters. Ask your characters what they think of current world events, when they lost their virginity, or if they've ever fired a weapon.

Every question answered reveals more about your character!

This worksheet is a great starting point for getting to know your characters—but only you know what questions are best to ask your creations. Answer the questions we've provided and then probe deeper.

Screenplay/Project: _____ Date: _____

Name: _____

Age: _____ Height: _____ Ethnicity: _____BL_____ ☐ Male ☒ Female

Nickname: _____ Clothing Style: _____

Hairstyle: _____ Eyewear: _____

Complexion: _____ Eye Color: _____ Hair Color: _____

Weight/Bodyshape: _____

Emotional Level: _____

Occupation: _____ Income: _____

Location: _____ Transportation: _____

Marital Status: _____

Children (number and names): _____

Family Information: _____

_____

_____

_____

Pets: _____ Political Party: _____

Nemesis: _____

Why: _____

Interest: _____

_____

_____

Quirks/Vices: _____

_____

_____

_____

Extra Information: _____

_____

_____

_____

_____

If you had a choice, who would play this character: _____

CHARACTER DEVELOPMENT WORKSHEET 2

Screenplay/Project: _____ Date: _____

Favorite Music Style: _____ Band: _____

Favorite Place to Visit: _____

Favorite Movie/Book: _____ Why: _____

Best Friend: _____ Why: _____

Favorite Number: _____ Favorite Food: _____ Least Favorite Food: _____

Allergies or Physical Handicaps: ☐ No ☐ Yes What: _____ How Long: _____

Chemical Dependency: ☐ No ☐ Yes For What: _____ How Long: _____

Criminal Past: ☐ No ☐ Yes For What: _____

Religious Beliefs: ☐ No ☐ Yes Faith: _____

Educational Level: _____

Oddest thing that has ever happened to him/her: _____

_____

_____

Personal goal yet achieved: _____

_____

Most afraid of: _____ Why: _____

_____

Greatest Strength: _____ Weakness: _____

Where does character see him/herself in 10 years: _____

_____

_____

Sexual Fantasy/Preference: _____

_____

Musically Inclinded: ☐ No ☐ Yes What Instrument: _____

Biggest Regret: _____ Why: _____

_____

Special Talents: _____

Any Family Traditions: ☐ No ☐ Yes What are they: _____

_____

Relate character to another movie persona: _____

Why: _____

Screenplay/Project: _____ Date: _____

Name:_____

Age: _____ Height: _____ Ethnicity: _____ ☐ Male ☐ Female

Nickname: _____ Clothing Style: _____

Hairstyle:_____ Eyewear:_____

Complexion: _____ Eye Color: _____ Hair Color: _____

Weight/Bodyshape:_____

Emotional Level: _____

Occupation: _____ Income:_____

Location: _____ Transportation:_____

Marital Status:_____

Children (number and names): _____

Family Information:_____

_____

_____

_____

Pets: _____ Political Party: _____

Nemesis:_____

Why:_____

Interest: _____

_____

_____

Quirks/Vices:_____

_____

_____

_____

Extra Information:_____

_____

_____

_____

If you had a choice, who would play this character: _____

The Screenplay Workbook

CHARACTER DEVELOPMENT WORKSHEET 2

Screenplay/Project: _____ Date: _____

Favorite Music Style: _____ Band: _____

Favorite Place to Visit: _____

Favorite Movie/Book: _____ Why: _____

Best Friend: _____ Why: _____

Favorite Number: _____ Favorite Food: _____ Least Favorite Food: _____

Allergies or Physical Handicaps: ☐ No ☐ Yes What: _____ How Long: _____

Chemical Dependency: ☐ No ☐ Yes For What: _____ How Long: _____

Criminal Past: ☐ No ☐ Yes For What: _____

Religious Beliefs: ☐ No ☐ Yes Faith: _____

Educational Level: _____

Oddest thing that has ever happened to him/her: _____

_____

_____

Personal goal yet achieved: _____

_____

Most afraid of: _____ Why: _____

_____

Greatest Strength: _____ Weakness: _____

Where does character see him/herself in 10 years: _____

_____

_____

Sexual Fantasy/Preference: _____

_____

Musically Inclinded: ☐ No ☐ Yes What Instrument: _____

Biggest Regret: _____ Why: _____

_____

Special Talents: _____

Any Family Traditions: ☐ No ☐ Yes What are they: _____

_____

Relate character to another movie persona: _____

Why: _____

The Screenplay Workbook

Screenplay/Project: _____ Date: _____

Name: _____

Age: _____ Height: _____ Ethnicity: _____ ☐ Male ☐ Female

Nickname: _____ Clothing Style: _____

Hairstyle: _____ Eyewear: _____

Complexion: _____ Eye Color: _____ Hair Color: _____

Weight/Bodyshape: _____

Emotional Level: _____

Occupation: _____ Income: _____

Location: _____ Transportation: _____

Marital Status: _____

Children (number and names): _____

Family Information: _____

_____

_____

_____

Pets: _____ Political Party: _____

Nemesis: _____

Why: _____

Interest: _____

_____

_____

Quirks/Vices: _____

_____

_____

_____

Extra Information: _____

_____

_____

_____

_____

If you had a choice, who would play this character: _____

The Screenplay Workbook

Screenplay/Project: _____ Date: _____

Favorite Music Style: _____ Band: _____

Favorite Place to Visit: _____

Favorite Movie/Book: _____ Why: _____

Best Friend: _____ Why: _____

Favorite Number: _____ Favorite Food: _____ Least Favorite Food: _____

Allergies or Physical Handicaps: ☐ No ☐ Yes What: _____ How Long: _____

Chemical Dependency: ☐ No ☐ Yes For What: _____ How Long: _____

Criminal Past: ☐ No ☐ Yes For What: _____

Religious Beliefs: ☐ No ☐ Yes Faith: _____

Educational Level: _____

Oddest thing that has ever happened to him/her: _____

_____

_____

Personal goal yet achieved: _____

_____

Most afraid of: _____ Why: _____

_____

Greatest Strength: _____ Weakness: _____

Where does character see him/herself in 10 years: _____

_____

_____

Sexual Fantasy/Preference: _____

_____

Musically Inclinded: ☐ No ☐ Yes What Instrument: _____

Biggest Regret: _____ Why: _____

_____

Special Talents: _____

Any Family Traditions: ☐ No ☐ Yes What are they: _____

_____

Relate character to another movie persona: _____

Why: _____

Screenplay/Project: _____ Date: _____

Name: _____

Age: _____ Height: _____ Ethnicity: _____ ☐ Male ☐ Female

Nickname: _____ Clothing Style: _____

Hairstyle: _____ Eyewear: _____

Complexion: _____ Eye Color: _____ Hair Color: _____

Weight/Bodyshape: _____

Emotional Level: _____

Occupation: _____ Income: _____

Location: _____ Transportation: _____

Marital Status: _____

Children (number and names): _____

Family Information: _____

_____

_____

_____

Pets: _____ Political Party: _____

Nemesis: _____

Why: _____

Interest: _____

_____

_____

Quirks/Vices: _____

_____

_____

_____

Extra Information: _____

_____

_____

_____

If you had a choice, who would play this character: _____

The Screenplay Workbook

CHARACTER DEVELOPMENT WORKSHEET 2

Screenplay/Project: _____ Date: _____

Favorite Music Style: _____ Band: _____

Favorite Place to Visit: _____

Favorite Movie/Book: _____ Why: _____

Best Friend: _____ Why: _____

Favorite Number: _____ Favorite Food: _____ Least Favorite Food: _____

Allergies or Physical Handicaps: ☐ No ☐ Yes What: _____ How Long: _____

Chemical Dependency: ☐ No ☐ Yes For What: _____ How Long: _____

Criminal Past: ☐ No ☐ Yes For What: _____

Religious Beliefs: ☐ No ☐ Yes Faith: _____

Educational Level: _____

Oddest thing that has ever happened to him/her: _____

_____

_____

Personal goal yet achieved: _____

_____

Most afraid of: _____ Why: _____

_____

Greatest Strength: _____ Weakness: _____

Where does character see him/herself in 10 years: _____

_____

_____

Sexual Fantasy/Preference: _____

_____

Musically Inclinded: ☐ No ☐ Yes What Instrument: _____

Biggest Regret: _____ Why: _____

_____

Special Talents: _____

Any Family Traditions: ☐ No ☐ Yes What are they: _____

_____

Relate character to another movie persona: _____

Why: _____

Screenplay/Project: _____ Date: _____

Name: _____

Age: _____ Height: _____ Ethnicity: _____ ☐ Male ☐ Female

Nickname: _____ Clothing Style: _____

Hairstyle: _____ Eyewear: _____

Complexion: _____ Eye Color: _____ Hair Color: _____

Weight/Bodyshape: _____

Emotional Level: _____

Occupation: _____ Income: _____

Location: _____ Transportation: _____

Marital Status: _____

Children (number and names): _____

Family Information: _____

_____

_____

_____

Pets: _____ Political Party: _____

Nemesis: _____

Why: _____

Interest: _____

_____

_____

Quirks/Vices: _____

_____

_____

_____

Extra Information: _____

_____

_____

_____

If you had a choice, who would play this character: _____

Screenplay/Project: _____ Date: _____

Favorite Music Style: _____ Band: _____

Favorite Place to Visit: _____

Favorite Movie/Book: _____ Why: _____

Best Friend: _____ Why: _____

Favorite Number: _____ Favorite Food: _____ Least Favorite Food: _____

Allergies or Physical Handicaps: ☐ No ☐ Yes What: _____ How Long: _____

Chemical Dependency: ☐ No ☐ Yes For What: _____ How Long: _____

Criminal Past: ☐ No ☐ Yes For What: _____

Religious Beliefs: ☐ No ☐ Yes Faith: _____

Educational Level: _____

Oddest thing that has ever happened to him/her: _____

_____

_____

Personal goal yet achieved: _____

_____

Most afraid of: _____ Why: _____

_____

Greatest Strength: _____ Weakness: _____

Where does character see him/herself in 10 years: _____

_____

_____

Sexual Fantasy/Preference: _____

_____

Musically Inclinded: ☐ No ☐ Yes What Instrument: _____

Biggest Regret: _____ Why: _____

_____

Special Talents: _____

Any Family Traditions: ☐ No ☐ Yes What are they: _____

_____

Relate character to another movie persona: _____

Why: _____

Screenplay/Project: _____ Date: _____

Name: _____

Age: _____ Height: _____ Ethnicity: _____ ☐ Male ☐ Female

Nickname: _____ Clothing Style: _____

Hairstyle: _____ Eyewear: _____

Complexion: _____ Eye Color: _____ Hair Color: _____

Weight/Bodyshape: _____

Emotional Level: _____

Occupation: _____ Income: _____

Location: _____ Transportation: _____

Marital Status: _____

Children (number and names): _____

Family Information: _____

_____

_____

_____

Pets: _____ Political Party: _____

Nemesis: _____

Why: _____

Interest: _____

_____

_____

Quirks/Vices: _____

_____

_____

_____

Extra Information: _____

_____

_____

_____

If you had a choice, who would play this character: _____

CHARACTER DEVELOPMENT WORKSHEET 2

Screenplay/Project: _____ Date: _____

Favorite Music Style: _____ Band: _____

Favorite Place to Visit: _____

Favorite Movie/Book: _____ Why: _____

Best Friend: _____ Why: _____

Favorite Number: _____ Favorite Food: _____ Least Favorite Food: _____

Allergies or Physical Handicaps: ☐ No ☐ Yes What: _____ How Long: _____

Chemical Dependency: ☐ No ☐ Yes For What: _____ How Long: _____

Criminal Past: ☐ No ☐ Yes For What: _____

Religious Beliefs: ☐ No ☐ Yes Faith: _____

Educational Level: _____

Oddest thing that has ever happened to him/her: _____

_____

_____

Personal goal yet achieved: _____

_____

Most afraid of: _____ Why: _____

_____

Greatest Strength: _____ Weakness: _____

Where does character see him/herself in 10 years: _____

_____

_____

Sexual Fantasy/Preference: _____

_____

Musically Inclinded: ☐ No ☐ Yes What Instrument: _____

Biggest Regret: _____ Why: _____

_____

Special Talents: _____

Any Family Traditions: ☐ No ☐ Yes What are they: _____

_____

Relate character to another movie persona: _____

Why: _____

Screenplay/Project: _____ Date: _____

Name: _____

Age: _____ Height: _____ Ethnicity: _____ ☐ Male ☐ Female

Nickname: _____ Clothing Style: _____

Hairstyle: _____ Eyewear: _____

Complexion: _____ Eye Color: _____ Hair Color: _____

Weight/Bodyshape: _____

Emotional Level: _____

Occupation: _____ Income: _____

Location: _____ Transportation: _____

Marital Status: _____

Children (number and names): _____

Family Information: _____

_____

_____

_____

Pets: _____ Political Party: _____

Nemesis: _____

Why: _____

Interest: _____

_____

_____

Quirks/Vices: _____

_____

_____

Extra Information: _____

_____

_____

_____

If you had a choice, who would play this character: _____

CHARACTER DEVELOPMENT WORKSHEET 2

Screenplay/Project: _____ Date: _____

Favorite Music Style: _____ Band: _____

Favorite Place to Visit: _____

Favorite Movie/Book: _____ Why: _____

Best Friend: _____ Why: _____

Favorite Number: _____ Favorite Food: _____ Least Favorite Food: _____

Allergies or Physical Handicaps: ☐ No ☐ Yes What: _____ How Long: _____

Chemical Dependency: ☐ No ☐ Yes For What: _____ How Long: _____

Criminal Past: ☐ No ☐ Yes For What: _____

Religious Beliefs: ☐ No ☐ Yes Faith: _____

Educational Level: _____

Oddest thing that has ever happened to him/her: _____

_____

_____

Personal goal yet achieved: _____

_____

Most afraid of: _____ Why: _____

_____

Greatest Strength: _____ Weakness: _____

Where does character see him/herself in 10 years: _____

_____

_____

Sexual Fantasy/Preference: _____

_____

Musically Inclinded: ☐ No ☐ Yes What Instrument: _____

Biggest Regret: _____ Why: _____

_____

Special Talents: _____

Any Family Traditions: ☐ No ☐ Yes What are they: _____

_____

Relate character to another movie persona: _____

Why: _____

Screenplay/Project: _____ Date: _____

Name: _____

Age: _____ Height: _____ Ethnicity: _____ ☐ Male ☐ Female

Nickname: _____ Clothing Style: _____

Hairstyle: _____ Eyewear: _____

Complexion: _____ Eye Color: _____ Hair Color: _____

Weight/Bodyshape: _____

Emotional Level: _____

Occupation: _____ Income: _____

Location: _____ Transportation: _____

Marital Status: _____

Children (number and names): _____

Family Information: _____

_____

_____

_____

Pets: _____ Political Party: _____

Nemesis: _____

Why: _____

Interest: _____

_____

_____

Quirks/Vices: _____

_____

_____

_____

Extra Information: _____

_____

_____

_____

_____

If you had a choice, who would play this character: _____

Screenplay/Project: _____ Date: _____

Favorite Music Style:_____ Band: _____

Favorite Place to Visit:_____

Favorite Movie/Book: _____ Why: _____

Best Friend: _____ Why: _____

Favorite Number: _____ Favorite Food: _____ Least Favorite Food:_____

Allergies or Physical Handicaps: ☐ No ☐ Yes What: _____ How Long: _____

Chemical Dependency: ☐ No ☐ Yes For What: _____ How Long: _____

Criminal Past: ☐ No ☐ Yes For What: _____

Religious Beliefs: ☐ No ☐ Yes Faith: _____

Educational Level:_____

Oddest thing that has ever happened to him/her: _____

_____

_____

Personal goal yet achieved: _____

_____

Most afraid of: _____ Why: _____

_____

Greatest Strength:_____ Weakness:_____

Where does character see him/herself in 10 years: _____

_____

_____

Sexual Fantasy/Preference: _____

_____

Musically Inclinded: ☐ No ☐ Yes What Instrument:_____

Biggest Regret:_____ Why: _____

_____

Special Talents: _____

Any Family Traditions: ☐ No ☐ Yes What are they: _____

_____

Relate character to another movie persona: _____

Why:_____

Screenplay/Project: _____   Date: _____

Name:_____

Age: _____   Height: _____   Ethnicity: _____   ☐ Male   ☐ Female

Nickname: _____   Clothing Style: _____

Hairstyle:_____   Eyewear:_____

Complexion: _____   Eye Color: _____   Hair Color: _____

Weight/Bodyshape:_____

Emotional Level: _____

Occupation: _____   Income:_____

Location: _____   Transportation:_____

Marital Status:_____

Children (number and names): _____

Family Information:_____

_____

_____

_____

Pets: _____   Political Party: _____

Nemesis:_____

Why:_____

Interest: _____

_____

_____

Quirks/Vices: _____

_____

_____

_____

Extra Information:_____

_____

_____

_____

_____

If you had a choice, who would play this character: _____

Screenplay/Project: _____ Date: _____

Favorite Music Style:_____ Band: _____

Favorite Place to Visit:_____

Favorite Movie/Book: _____ Why: _____

Best Friend: _____ Why: _____

Favorite Number: _____ Favorite Food: _____ Least Favorite Food:_____

Allergies or Physical Handicaps: ☐ No ☐ Yes What: _____ How Long: _____

Chemical Dependency: ☐ No ☐ Yes For What: _____ How Long: _____

Criminal Past: ☐ No ☐ Yes For What: _____

Religious Beliefs: ☐ No ☐ Yes Faith: _____

Educational Level:_____

Oddest thing that has ever happened to him/her: _____

_____

_____

Personal goal yet achieved: _____

_____

Most afraid of: _____ Why: _____

_____

Greatest Strength:_____ Weakness:_____

Where does character see him/herself in 10 years: _____

_____

_____

Sexual Fantasy/Preference: _____

_____

Musically Inclinded: ☐ No ☐ Yes What Instrument:_____

Biggest Regret:_____ Why: _____

_____

Special Talents: _____

Any Family Traditions: ☐ No ☐ Yes What are they: _____

_____

Relate character to another movie persona: _____

Why:_____

CHARACTER DEVELOPMENT WORKSHEET 1

Screenplay/Project: _____   Date: _____

Name: _____

Age: _____   Height: _____   Ethnicity: _____   ☐ Male   ☐ Female

Nickname: _____   Clothing Style: _____

Hairstyle: _____   Eyewear: _____

Complexion: _____   Eye Color: _____   Hair Color: _____

Weight/Bodyshape: _____

Emotional Level: _____

Occupation: _____   Income: _____

Location: _____   Transportation: _____

Marital Status: _____

Children (number and names): _____

Family Information: _____

_____

_____

_____

Pets: _____   Political Party: _____

Nemesis: _____

Why: _____

Interest: _____

_____

_____

Quirks/Vices: _____

_____

_____

_____

Extra Information: _____

_____

_____

_____

_____

If you had a choice, who would play this character: _____

Screenplay/Project: _____ Date: _____

Favorite Music Style:_____ Band: _____

Favorite Place to Visit:_____

Favorite Movie/Book: _____ Why: _____

Best Friend: _____ Why: _____

Favorite Number: _____   Favorite Food: _____   Least Favorite Food:_____

Allergies or Physical Handicaps: ☐ No   ☐ Yes   What: _____   How Long: _____

Chemical Dependency: ☐ No   ☐ Yes   For What: _____   How Long: _____

Criminal Past: ☐ No   ☐ Yes   For What: _____

Religious Beliefs: ☐ No   ☐ Yes   Faith: _____

Educational Level:_____

Oddest thing that has ever happened to him/her: _____

_____

_____

Personal goal yet achieved: _____

_____

Most afraid of: _____ Why: _____

_____

Greatest Strength:_____ Weakness:_____

Where does character see him/herself in 10 years: _____

_____

_____

Sexual Fantasy/Preference: _____

_____

Musically Inclinded: ☐ No   ☐ Yes   What Instrument:_____

Biggest Regret:_____ Why: _____

_____

Special Talents: _____

Any Family Traditions: ☐ No   ☐ Yes   What are they: _____

_____

Relate character to another movie persona: _____

Why:_____

Screenplay/Project: _____   Date: _____

Name: _____

Age: _____   Height: _____   Ethnicity: _____   ☐ Male   ☐ Female

Nickname: _____   Clothing Style: _____

Hairstyle: _____   Eyewear: _____

Complexion: _____   Eye Color: _____   Hair Color: _____

Weight/Bodyshape: _____

Emotional Level: _____

Occupation: _____   Income: _____

Location: _____   Transportation: _____

Marital Status: _____

Children (number and names): _____

Family Information: _____

_____

_____

_____

Pets: _____   Political Party: _____

Nemesis: _____

Why: _____

Interest: _____

_____

_____

Quirks/Vices: _____

_____

_____

_____

Extra Information: _____

_____

_____

_____

_____

If you had a choice, who would play this character: _____

Screenplay/Project: _____ Date: _____

Favorite Music Style: _____ Band: _____

Favorite Place to Visit: _____

Favorite Movie/Book: _____ Why: _____

Best Friend: _____ Why: _____

Favorite Number: _____ Favorite Food: _____ Least Favorite Food: _____

Allergies or Physical Handicaps: ☐ No ☐ Yes What: _____ How Long: _____

Chemical Dependency: ☐ No ☐ Yes For What: _____ How Long: _____

Criminal Past: ☐ No ☐ Yes For What: _____

Religious Beliefs: ☐ No ☐ Yes Faith: _____

Educational Level: _____

Oddest thing that has ever happened to him/her: _____
_____
_____

Personal goal yet achieved: _____
_____

Most afraid of: _____ Why: _____
_____

Greatest Strength: _____ Weakness: _____

Where does character see him/herself in 10 years: _____
_____
_____

Sexual Fantasy/Preference: _____
_____

Musically Inclinded: ☐ No ☐ Yes What Instrument: _____

Biggest Regret: _____ Why: _____
_____

Special Talents: _____

Any Family Traditions: ☐ No ☐ Yes What are they: _____
_____

Relate character to another movie persona: _____

Why: _____

CHARACTER DEVELOPMENT WORKSHEET 1

Screenplay/Project: _____ Date: _____

Name: _____

Age: _____ Height: _____ Ethnicity: _____ ☐ Male ☐ Female

Nickname: _____ Clothing Style: _____

Hairstyle: _____ Eyewear: _____

Complexion: _____ Eye Color: _____ Hair Color: _____

Weight/Bodyshape: _____

Emotional Level: _____

Occupation: _____ Income: _____

Location: _____ Transportation: _____

Marital Status: _____

Children (number and names): _____

Family Information: _____

_____

_____

_____

Pets: _____ Political Party: _____

Nemesis: _____

Why: _____

Interest: _____

_____

_____

Quirks/Vices: _____

_____

_____

_____

Extra Information: _____

_____

_____

_____

_____

If you had a choice, who would play this character: _____

Screenplay/Project: _____ Date: _____

Favorite Music Style:_____ Band: _____

Favorite Place to Visit:_____

Favorite Movie/Book: _____ Why: _____

Best Friend: _____ Why: _____

Favorite Number: _____   Favorite Food: _____ Least Favorite Food:_____

Allergies or Physical Handicaps: ☐ No   ☐ Yes   What: _____ How Long: _____

Chemical Dependency: ☐ No   ☐ Yes   For What: _____ How Long: _____

Criminal Past: ☐ No   ☐ Yes   For What: _____

Religious Beliefs: ☐ No   ☐ Yes   Faith: _____

Educational Level:_____

Oddest thing that has ever happened to him/her: _____

_____

_____

Personal goal yet achieved: _____

_____

Most afraid of: _____ Why: _____

_____

Greatest Strength:_____ Weakness:_____

Where does character see him/herself in 10 years: _____

_____

_____

Sexual Fantasy/Preference: _____

_____

Musically Inclinded: ☐ No   ☐ Yes   What Instrument:_____

Biggest Regret:_____ Why: _____

_____

Special Talents: _____

Any Family Traditions: ☐ No   ☐ Yes   What are they: _____

_____

Relate character to another movie persona: _____

Why:_____

 **The Screenplay Workbook**

CHARACTER DEVELOPMENT WORKSHEET 1

Screenplay/Project: _____ Date: _____

Name:_____

Age: _____ Height: _____ Ethnicity: _____ ☐ Male ☐ Female

Nickname: _____ Clothing Style: _____

Hairstyle:_____ Eyewear:_____

Complexion: _____ Eye Color: _____ Hair Color: _____

Weight/Bodyshape:_____

Emotional Level:_____

Occupation: _____ Income:_____

Location: _____ Transportation:_____

Marital Status:_____

Children (number and names): _____

Family Information:_____

_____

_____

_____

Pets: _____ Political Party: _____

Nemesis:_____

Why:_____

Interest: _____

_____

_____

Quirks/Vices: _____

_____

_____

Extra Information:_____

_____

_____

_____

_____

If you had a choice, who would play this character: _____

Screenplay/Project: _____ Date: _____

Favorite Music Style: _____ Band: _____

Favorite Place to Visit: _____

Favorite Movie/Book: _____ Why: _____

Best Friend: _____ Why: _____

Favorite Number: _____ Favorite Food: _____ Least Favorite Food: _____

Allergies or Physical Handicaps: ☐ No ☐ Yes What: _____ How Long: _____

Chemical Dependency: ☐ No ☐ Yes For What: _____ How Long: _____

Criminal Past: ☐ No ☐ Yes For What: _____

Religious Beliefs: ☐ No ☐ Yes Faith: _____

Educational Level: _____

Oddest thing that has ever happened to him/her: _____

_____

_____

Personal goal yet achieved: _____

_____

Most afraid of: _____ Why: _____

_____

Greatest Strength: _____ Weakness: _____

Where does character see him/herself in 10 years: _____

_____

_____

Sexual Fantasy/Preference: _____

_____

Musically Inclinded: ☐ No ☐ Yes What Instrument: _____

Biggest Regret: _____ Why: _____

_____

Special Talents: _____

Any Family Traditions: ☐ No ☐ Yes What are they: _____

_____

Relate character to another movie persona: _____

Why: _____

Screenplay/Project: _____ Date: _____

Name: _____

Age: _____ Height: _____ Ethnicity: _____ ☐ Male ☐ Female

Nickname: _____ Clothing Style: _____

Hairstyle: _____ Eyewear: _____

Complexion: _____ Eye Color: _____ Hair Color: _____

Weight/Bodyshape: _____

Emotional Level: _____

Occupation: _____ Income: _____

Location: _____ Transportation: _____

Marital Status: _____

Children (number and names): _____

Family Information: _____

_____

_____

_____

Pets: _____ Political Party: _____

Nemesis: _____

Why: _____

Interest: _____

_____

_____

Quirks/Vices: _____

_____

_____

Extra Information: _____

_____

_____

_____

_____

If you had a choice, who would play this character: _____

Screenplay/Project: _____ Date: _____

Favorite Music Style:_____ Band: _____

Favorite Place to Visit:_____

Favorite Movie/Book: _____ Why: _____

Best Friend: _____ Why: _____

Favorite Number: _____ Favorite Food: _____ Least Favorite Food:_____

Allergies or Physical Handicaps: ☐ No ☐ Yes What: _____ How Long: _____

Chemical Dependency: ☐ No ☐ Yes For What: _____ How Long: _____

Criminal Past: ☐ No ☐ Yes For What: _____

Religious Beliefs: ☐ No ☐ Yes Faith: _____

Educational Level:_____

Oddest thing that has ever happened to him/her: _____

_____

_____

Personal goal yet achieved: _____

_____

Most afraid of: _____ Why: _____

_____

Greatest Strength:_____ Weakness:_____

Where does character see him/herself in 10 years: _____

_____

_____

Sexual Fantasy/Preference: _____

_____

Musically Inclinded: ☐ No ☐ Yes What Instrument:_____

Biggest Regret:_____ Why: _____

_____

Special Talents: _____

Any Family Traditions: ☐ No ☐ Yes What are they: _____

_____

Relate character to another movie persona: _____

Why:_____

Screenplay/Project: _____ Date: _____

Name: _____

Age: _____ Height: _____ Ethnicity: _____ ☐ Male ☐ Female

Nickname: _____ Clothing Style: _____

Hairstyle: _____ Eyewear: _____

Complexion: _____ Eye Color: _____ Hair Color: _____

Weight/Bodyshape: _____

Emotional Level: _____

Occupation: _____ Income: _____

Location: _____ Transportation: _____

Marital Status: _____

Children (number and names): _____

Family Information: _____

_____

_____

_____

Pets: _____ Political Party: _____

Nemesis: _____

Why: _____

Interest: _____

_____

_____

Quirks/Vices: _____

_____

_____

_____

Extra Information: _____

_____

_____

_____

_____

If you had a choice, who would play this character: _____

Screenplay/Project: _____ Date: _____

Favorite Music Style: _____ Band: _____

Favorite Place to Visit: _____

Favorite Movie/Book: _____ Why: _____

Best Friend: _____ Why: _____

Favorite Number: _____ Favorite Food: _____ Least Favorite Food: _____

Allergies or Physical Handicaps: ☐ No ☐ Yes What: _____ How Long: _____

Chemical Dependency: ☐ No ☐ Yes For What: _____ How Long: _____

Criminal Past: ☐ No ☐ Yes For What: _____

Religious Beliefs: ☐ No ☐ Yes Faith: _____

Educational Level: _____

Oddest thing that has ever happened to him/her: _____

_____

_____

Personal goal yet achieved: _____

_____

Most afraid of: _____ Why: _____

_____

Greatest Strength: _____ Weakness: _____

Where does character see him/herself in 10 years: _____

_____

_____

Sexual Fantasy/Preference: _____

_____

Musically Inclinded: ☐ No ☐ Yes What Instrument: _____

Biggest Regret: _____ Why: _____

_____

Special Talents: _____

Any Family Traditions: ☐ No ☐ Yes What are they: _____

_____

Relate character to another movie persona: _____

Why: _____

Screenplay/Project: _____   Date: _____

Name: _____

Age: _____   Height: _____   Ethnicity: _____   ☐ Male   ☐ Female

Nickname: _____   Clothing Style: _____

Hairstyle: _____   Eyewear: _____

Complexion: _____   Eye Color: _____   Hair Color: _____

Weight/Bodyshape: _____

Emotional Level: _____

Occupation: _____   Income: _____

Location: _____   Transportation: _____

Marital Status: _____

Children (number and names): _____

Family Information: _____

_____

_____

_____

Pets: _____   Political Party: _____

Nemesis: _____

Why: _____

Interest: _____

_____

_____

Quirks/Vices: _____

_____

_____

_____

Extra Information: _____

_____

_____

_____

_____

If you had a choice, who would play this character: _____

CHARACTER DEVELOPMENT WORKSHEET 2

Screenplay/Project: _____ Date: _____

Favorite Music Style: _____ Band: _____

Favorite Place to Visit: _____

Favorite Movie/Book: _____ Why: _____

Best Friend: _____ Why: _____

Favorite Number: _____ Favorite Food: _____ Least Favorite Food: _____

Allergies or Physical Handicaps: ☐ No ☐ Yes What: _____ How Long: _____

Chemical Dependency: ☐ No ☐ Yes For What: _____ How Long: _____

Criminal Past: ☐ No ☐ Yes For What: _____

Religious Beliefs: ☐ No ☐ Yes Faith: _____

Educational Level: _____

Oddest thing that has ever happened to him/her: _____

_____

_____

Personal goal yet achieved: _____

_____

Most afraid of: _____ Why: _____

_____

Greatest Strength: _____ Weakness: _____

Where does character see him/herself in 10 years: _____

_____

_____

Sexual Fantasy/Preference: _____

_____

Musically Inclinded: ☐ No ☐ Yes What Instrument: _____

Biggest Regret: _____ Why: _____

_____

Special Talents: _____

Any Family Traditions: ☐ No ☐ Yes What are they: _____

_____

Relate character to another movie persona: _____

Why: _____

Screenplay/Project: _____ Date: _____

Name: _____

Age: _____ Height: _____ Ethnicity: _____ ☐ Male ☐ Female

Nickname: _____ Clothing Style: _____

Hairstyle: _____ Eyewear: _____

Complexion: _____ Eye Color: _____ Hair Color: _____

Weight/Bodyshape: _____

Emotional Level: _____

Occupation: _____ Income: _____

Location: _____ Transportation: _____

Marital Status: _____

Children (number and names): _____

Family Information: _____

_____

_____

_____

Pets: _____ Political Party: _____

Nemesis: _____

Why: _____

Interest: _____

_____

_____

Quirks/Vices: _____

_____

_____

_____

Extra Information: _____

_____

_____

_____

If you had a choice, who would play this character: _____

Screenplay/Project: _____ Date: _____

Favorite Music Style: _____ Band: _____

Favorite Place to Visit: _____

Favorite Movie/Book: _____ Why: _____

Best Friend: _____ Why: _____

Favorite Number: _____ Favorite Food: _____ Least Favorite Food: _____

Allergies or Physical Handicaps: ☐ No ☐ Yes What: _____ How Long: _____

Chemical Dependency: ☐ No ☐ Yes For What: _____ How Long: _____

Criminal Past: ☐ No ☐ Yes For What: _____

Religious Beliefs: ☐ No ☐ Yes Faith: _____

Educational Level: _____

Oddest thing that has ever happened to him/her: _____

_____

_____

Personal goal yet achieved: _____

_____

Most afraid of: _____ Why: _____

_____

Greatest Strength: _____ Weakness: _____

Where does character see him/herself in 10 years: _____

_____

_____

Sexual Fantasy/Preference: _____

_____

Musically Inclinded: ☐ No ☐ Yes What Instrument: _____

Biggest Regret: _____ Why: _____

_____

Special Talents: _____

Any Family Traditions: ☐ No ☐ Yes What are they: _____

_____

Relate character to another movie persona: _____

Why: _____

Screenplay/Project: _____ Date: _____

Name: _____

Age: _____ Height: _____ Ethnicity: _____ ☐ Male ☐ Female

Nickname: _____ Clothing Style: _____

Hairstyle: _____ Eyewear: _____

Complexion: _____ Eye Color: _____ Hair Color: _____

Weight/Bodyshape: _____

Emotional Level: _____

Occupation: _____ Income: _____

Location: _____ Transportation: _____

Marital Status: _____

Children (number and names): _____

Family Information: _____

_____

_____

_____

Pets: _____ Political Party: _____

Nemesis: _____

Why: _____

Interest: _____

_____

_____

Quirks/Vices: _____

_____

_____

Extra Information: _____

_____

_____

_____

_____

If you had a choice, who would play this character: _____

Screenplay/Project: _____ Date: _____

Favorite Music Style: _____ Band: _____

Favorite Place to Visit: _____

Favorite Movie/Book: _____ Why: _____

Best Friend: _____ Why: _____

Favorite Number: _____ Favorite Food: _____ Least Favorite Food: _____

Allergies or Physical Handicaps: ☐ No ☐ Yes What: _____ How Long: _____

Chemical Dependency: ☐ No ☐ Yes For What: _____ How Long: _____

Criminal Past: ☐ No ☐ Yes For What: _____

Religious Beliefs: ☐ No ☐ Yes Faith: _____

Educational Level: _____

Oddest thing that has ever happened to him/her: _____

_____

_____

Personal goal yet achieved: _____

_____

Most afraid of: _____ Why: _____

_____

Greatest Strength: _____ Weakness: _____

Where does character see him/herself in 10 years: _____

_____

_____

Sexual Fantasy/Preference: _____

_____

Musically Inclinded: ☐ No ☐ Yes What Instrument: _____

Biggest Regret: _____ Why: _____

_____

Special Talents: _____

Any Family Traditions: ☐ No ☐ Yes What are they: _____

_____

Relate character to another movie persona: _____

Why: _____

Screenplay/Project: _____ Date: _____

Name: _____

Age: _____ Height: _____ Ethnicity: _____ ☐ Male ☐ Female

Nickname: _____ Clothing Style: _____

Hairstyle: _____ Eyewear: _____

Complexion: _____ Eye Color: _____ Hair Color: _____

Weight/Bodyshape: _____

Emotional Level: _____

Occupation: _____ Income: _____

Location: _____ Transportation: _____

Marital Status: _____

Children (number and names): _____

Family Information: _____

_____

_____

_____

Pets: _____ Political Party: _____

Nemesis: _____

Why: _____

Interest: _____

_____

_____

Quirks/Vices: _____

_____

_____

_____

Extra Information: _____

_____

_____

_____

If you had a choice, who would play this character: _____

Screenplay/Project: _____ Date: _____

Favorite Music Style: _____ Band: _____

Favorite Place to Visit: _____

Favorite Movie/Book: _____ Why: _____

Best Friend: _____ Why: _____

Favorite Number: _____ Favorite Food: _____ Least Favorite Food: _____

Allergies or Physical Handicaps: ☐ No ☐ Yes What: _____ How Long: _____

Chemical Dependency: ☐ No ☐ Yes For What: _____ How Long: _____

Criminal Past: ☐ No ☐ Yes For What: _____

Religious Beliefs: ☐ No ☐ Yes Faith: _____

Educational Level: _____

Oddest thing that has ever happened to him/her: _____

_____

_____

Personal goal yet achieved: _____

_____

Most afraid of: _____ Why: _____

_____

Greatest Strength: _____ Weakness: _____

Where does character see him/herself in 10 years: _____

_____

_____

Sexual Fantasy/Preference: _____

_____

Musically Inclinded: ☐ No ☐ Yes What Instrument: _____

Biggest Regret: _____ Why: _____

_____

Special Talents: _____

Any Family Traditions: ☐ No ☐ Yes What are they: _____

_____

Relate character to another movie persona: _____

Why: _____

Screenplay/Project: _____ Date: _____

Name: _____

Age: _____   Height: _____   Ethnicity: _____   ☐ Male   ☐ Female

Nickname: _____   Clothing Style: _____

Hairstyle: _____   Eyewear: _____

Complexion: _____   Eye Color: _____   Hair Color: _____

Weight/Bodyshape: _____

Emotional Level: _____

Occupation: _____   Income: _____

Location: _____   Transportation: _____

Marital Status: _____

Children (number and names): _____

Family Information: _____

_____

_____

_____

Pets: _____   Political Party: _____

Nemesis: _____

Why: _____

Interest: _____

_____

_____

Quirks/Vices: _____

_____

_____

_____

Extra Information: _____

_____

_____

_____

If you had a choice, who would play this character: _____

Screenplay/Project: _____ Date: _____

Favorite Music Style: _____ Band: _____

Favorite Place to Visit: _____

Favorite Movie/Book: _____ Why: _____

Best Friend: _____ Why: _____

Favorite Number: _____ Favorite Food: _____ Least Favorite Food: _____

Allergies or Physical Handicaps: ☐ No ☐ Yes What: _____ How Long: _____

Chemical Dependency: ☐ No ☐ Yes For What: _____ How Long: _____

Criminal Past: ☐ No ☐ Yes For What: _____

Religious Beliefs: ☐ No ☐ Yes Faith: _____

Educational Level: _____

Oddest thing that has ever happened to him/her: _____

_____

_____

Personal goal yet achieved: _____

_____

Most afraid of: _____ Why: _____

_____

Greatest Strength: _____ Weakness: _____

Where does character see him/herself in 10 years: _____

_____

_____

Sexual Fantasy/Preference: _____

_____

Musically Inclinded: ☐ No ☐ Yes What Instrument: _____

Biggest Regret: _____ Why: _____

_____

Special Talents: _____

Any Family Traditions: ☐ No ☐ Yes What are they: _____

_____

Relate character to another movie persona: _____

Why: _____

Screenplay/Project: _____ Date: _____

Name: _____

Age: _____ Height: _____ Ethnicity: _____ ☐ Male ☐ Female

Nickname: _____ Clothing Style: _____

Hairstyle: _____ Eyewear: _____

Complexion: _____ Eye Color: _____ Hair Color: _____

Weight/Bodyshape: _____

Emotional Level: _____

Occupation: _____ Income: _____

Location: _____ Transportation: _____

Marital Status: _____

Children (number and names): _____

Family Information: _____

_____

_____

_____

Pets: _____ Political Party: _____

Nemesis: _____

Why: _____

Interest: _____

_____

_____

Quirks/Vices: _____

_____

_____

_____

Extra Information: _____

_____

_____

_____

_____

If you had a choice, who would play this character: _____

Screenplay/Project: _____ Date: _____

Favorite Music Style:_____ Band: _____

Favorite Place to Visit:_____

Favorite Movie/Book: _____ Why: _____

Best Friend: _____ Why: _____

Favorite Number: _____ Favorite Food:_____ Least Favorite Food:_____

Allergies or Physical Handicaps: ☐ No ☐ Yes What: _____ How Long: _____

Chemical Dependency: ☐ No ☐ Yes For What: _____ How Long: _____

Criminal Past: ☐ No ☐ Yes For What: _____

Religious Beliefs: ☐ No ☐ Yes Faith: _____

Educational Level:_____

Oddest thing that has ever happened to him/her: _____

_____

_____

Personal goal yet achieved: _____

_____

Most afraid of: _____ Why: _____

_____

Greatest Strength:_____ Weakness:_____

Where does character see him/herself in 10 years: _____

_____

_____

Sexual Fantasy/Preference: _____

_____

Musically Inclinded: ☐ No ☐ Yes What Instrument:_____

Biggest Regret:_____ Why: _____

_____

Special Talents: _____

Any Family Traditions: ☐ No ☐ Yes What are they: _____

_____

Relate character to another movie persona: _____

Why:_____

CHARACTER DEVELOPMENT WORKSHEET 1

Screenplay/Project: _____ Date: _____

Name: _____

Age: _____ Height: _____ Ethnicity: _____ ☐ Male ☐ Female

Nickname: _____ Clothing Style: _____

Hairstyle: _____ Eyewear: _____

Complexion: _____ Eye Color: _____ Hair Color: _____

Weight/Bodyshape: _____

Emotional Level: _____

Occupation: _____ Income: _____

Location: _____ Transportation: _____

Marital Status: _____

Children (number and names): _____

Family Information: _____

_____

_____

_____

Pets: _____ Political Party: _____

Nemesis: _____

Why: _____

Interest: _____

_____

_____

Quirks/Vices: _____

_____

_____

_____

Extra Information: _____

_____

_____

_____

_____

If you had a choice, who would play this character: _____

Screenplay/Project: _____   Date: _____

Favorite Music Style:_____   Band: _____

Favorite Place to Visit:_____

Favorite Movie/Book: _____   Why: _____

Best Friend: _____   Why: _____

Favorite Number: _____   Favorite Food:_____   Least Favorite Food:_____

Allergies or Physical Handicaps: ☐ No ☐ Yes   What: _____   How Long: _____

Chemical Dependency: ☐ No ☐ Yes   For What: _____   How Long: _____

Criminal Past: ☐ No ☐ Yes   For What: _____

Religious Beliefs: ☐ No ☐ Yes   Faith: _____

Educational Level:_____

Oddest thing that has ever happened to him/her: _____

_____

_____

Personal goal yet achieved: _____

_____

Most afraid of: _____   Why: _____

_____

Greatest Strength:_____   Weakness:_____

Where does character see him/herself in 10 years: _____

_____

_____

Sexual Fantasy/Preference: _____

_____

Musically Inclinded: ☐ No ☐ Yes   What Instrument:_____

Biggest Regret:_____   Why: _____

_____

Special Talents: _____

Any Family Traditions: ☐ No ☐ Yes   What are they: _____

_____

Relate character to another movie persona: _____

Why:_____

Screenplay/Project: _____ Date: _____

Name:_____

Age: _____ Height: _____ Ethnicity: _____ ☐ Male ☐ Female

Nickname: _____ Clothing Style: _____

Hairstyle:_____ Eyewear:_____

Complexion: _____ Eye Color: _____ Hair Color: _____

Weight/Bodyshape:_____

Emotional Level:_____

Occupation: _____ Income:_____

Location: _____ Transportation:_____

Marital Status:_____

Children (number and names): _____

Family Information:_____

_____

_____

_____

Pets: _____ Political Party: _____

Nemesis: _____

Why:_____

Interest: _____

_____

_____

Quirks/Vices: _____

_____

_____

_____

Extra Information:_____

_____

_____

_____

_____

If you had a choice, who would play this character: _____

Screenplay/Project: _____   Date: _____

Favorite Music Style:_____   Band: _____

Favorite Place to Visit:_____

Favorite Movie/Book: _____   Why: _____

Best Friend: _____   Why: _____

Favorite Number: _____   Favorite Food: _____   Least Favorite Food:_____

Allergies or Physical Handicaps: ☐ No   ☐ Yes   What: _____   How Long: _____

Chemical Dependency: ☐ No   ☐ Yes   For What: _____   How Long: _____

Criminal Past: ☐ No   ☐ Yes   For What: _____

Religious Beliefs: ☐ No   ☐ Yes   Faith: _____

Educational Level:_____

Oddest thing that has ever happened to him/her: _____

_____

_____

Personal goal yet achieved: _____

_____

Most afraid of: _____   Why: _____

_____

Greatest Strength:_____   Weakness:_____

Where does character see him/herself in 10 years: _____

_____

_____

Sexual Fantasy/Preference: _____

_____

Musically Inclinded: ☐ No   ☐ Yes   What Instrument:_____

Biggest Regret:_____   Why: _____

_____

Special Talents: _____

Any Family Traditions: ☐ No   ☐ Yes   What are they: _____

_____

Relate character to another movie persona: _____

Why:_____

CHARACTER DEVELOPMENT WORKSHEET 1

Screenplay/Project: _____ Date: _____

Name: _____

Age: _____ Height: _____ Ethnicity: _____ ☐ Male ☐ Female

Nickname: _____ Clothing Style: _____

Hairstyle: _____ Eyewear: _____

Complexion: _____ Eye Color: _____ Hair Color: _____

Weight/Bodyshape: _____

Emotional Level: _____

Occupation: _____ Income: _____

Location: _____ Transportation: _____

Marital Status: _____

Children (number and names): _____

Family Information: _____

_____

_____

_____

Pets: _____ Political Party: _____

Nemesis: _____

Why: _____

Interest: _____

_____

_____

Quirks/Vices: _____

_____

_____

_____

Extra Information: _____

_____

_____

_____

_____

If you had a choice, who would play this character: _____

Screenplay/Project: _____   Date: _____

Favorite Music Style:_____   Band: _____

Favorite Place to Visit:_____

Favorite Movie/Book: _____   Why: _____

Best Friend: _____   Why: _____

Favorite Number: _____   Favorite Food: _____   Least Favorite Food:_____

Allergies or Physical Handicaps: ☐ No   ☐ Yes   What: _____   How Long: _____

Chemical Dependency: ☐ No   ☐ Yes   For What: _____   How Long: _____

Criminal Past: ☐ No   ☐ Yes   For What: _____

Religious Beliefs: ☐ No   ☐ Yes   Faith: _____

Educational Level:_____

Oddest thing that has ever happened to him/her: _____

_____

_____

Personal goal yet achieved: _____

_____

Most afraid of: _____   Why: _____

_____

Greatest Strength._____   Weakness._____

Where does character see him/herself in 10 years: _____

_____

_____

Sexual Fantasy/Preference: _____

_____

Musically Inclinded: ☐ No   ☐ Yes   What Instrument:_____

Biggest Regret:_____   Why: _____

_____

Special Talents: _____

Any Family Traditions: ☐ No   ☐ Yes   What are they: _____

_____

Relate character to another movie persona: _____

Why:_____

 **CHARACTER DEVELOPMENT WORKSHEET 1**

Screenplay/Project: _____ Date: _____

Name: _____

Age: _____ Height: _____ Ethnicity: _____ ☐ Male ☐ Female

Nickname: _____ Clothing Style: _____

Hairstyle: _____ Eyewear: _____

Complexion: _____ Eye Color: _____ Hair Color: _____

Weight/Bodyshape: _____

Emotional Level: _____

Occupation: _____ Income: _____

Location: _____ Transportation: _____

Marital Status: _____

Children (number and names): _____

Family Information: _____

_____

_____

_____

Pets: _____ Political Party: _____

Nemesis: _____

Why: _____

Interest: _____

_____

_____

Quirks/Vices: _____

_____

_____

_____

Extra Information: _____

_____

_____

_____

_____

If you had a choice, who would play this character: _____

Screenplay/Project: _____ Date: _____

Favorite Music Style:_____ Band: _____

Favorite Place to Visit:_____

Favorite Movie/Book: _____ Why: _____

Best Friend: _____ Why: _____

Favorite Number: _____ Favorite Food:_____ Least Favorite Food:_____

Allergies or Physical Handicaps: ☐ No ☐ Yes What: _____ How Long: _____

Chemical Dependency: ☐ No ☐ Yes For What: _____ How Long: _____

Criminal Past: ☐ No ☐ Yes For What: _____

Religious Beliefs: ☐ No ☐ Yes Faith: _____

Educational Level:_____

Oddest thing that has ever happened to him/her: _____

_____

_____

Personal goal yet achieved: _____

_____

Most afraid of: _____ Why: _____

_____

Greatest Strength:_____ Weakness:_____

Where does character see him/herself in 10 years: _____

_____

_____

Sexual Fantasy/Preference: _____

_____

Musically Inclinded: ☐ No ☐ Yes What Instrument:_____

Biggest Regret:_____ Why: _____

_____

Special Talents: _____

Any Family Traditions: ☐ No ☐ Yes What are they: _____

_____

Relate character to another movie persona: _____

Why:_____

John would later discover that basing his new characters on phone conversations with his mother was a very bad idea.

Chapter 4

CHARACTER RELATIONSHIPS

Unless you are a hermit living in isolation, you have relationships. And so should your characters. While the most important relationship in your screenplay should be between your protagonist and antagonist, every character who interacts with another creates a relationship. You should know every possible conversation point, disagreement, similarity, etc, that your characters may have when they interact with each other.

Well-defined relationships make your characters believable and well-rounded. In every aspect of our lives, there are details we know about others that shape the way we act, talk and sometimes even think.

EXAMPLE #1: Some people are easily offended by cursing. When you know someone is offended by cursing, do you continue to curse in their presence, or do you wait until they're gone? A character prone to cursing would most likely stop cursing when speaking to another character offended by foul language. It's what real people do. It's what good characters should do (unless they don't care that they're offending other characters, or if being offensive is their goal).

EXAMPLE #2: Brian and Kevin are best friends. They play G.I. Joes every Saturday morning, walk to school together every day, and are on the same soccer team. If you pick a fight with one of them, you pick a fight with both of them. But Brian has a secret side, borrowing other kid's toys, pretending to lose them and keeping them for himself. He's amassed an impressive collection.

Kevin, being the trusting friend, lets Brian borrow his treasured, vintage *Millennium Falcon*. Weeks pass and while Kevin hasn't asked for the toy back, Brian has yet to return it. On the way to Brian's house to ask for the Falcon, Kevin grabs a Coke at the 7/11 and bumps into Stu, a mutual friend of his and Brian, who also happens to be one of Brian's victims. Stu complains about his missing toy and tells Kevin about all the kids who let Brian borrow a toy, only to never get it back.

What happens next? Does Kevin rush back home, fearing he'll never see his Millennium Falcon again? Does he still trust Brian with his toys, but feel betrayed? Does he search Brian's room for the missing toys and after a showdown with the evil Brian, turn him in to Mom? If you know that all this happened, previous to the beginning of your story, Brian and Kevin's onscreen relationship will be tangible.

EXAMPLE #3: Superman and Lex Luther. What are their ultimate goals? Superman wants to protect the citizens of Earth from harm. He stands for truth, justice and the American way. Lex wants to rule the world through death, betrayal and destruction. The two characters a pitted against each other from the onset. But what if this information was concealed? The *Smallville* series on the WB network turned the classic story of Superman and Lex Luther in a new direction, with both characters naïve to who the other will eventually become. The average person knows that Lex and Clark will become archenemies, and in this case, the knowledge of their future relationship is extremely powerful. When you create your characters, try to envision their relationships in past, present and future. It may take your story in new and exciting directions.

Use the Character Relationships worksheet as a comparison chart. Fill out each side for characters who interact in your story and see what kind of differences, problems and similarities arise. You should find that your characters interact better and on a more believable level.

JEREMY'S INSIDE SCOOP

What does every screenwriter have in common? Rejection. But how individual screenwriters handle that rejection varies drastically. Here's how you should handle rejection: suck it up, take it, apply any comments and move forward. You got rejected for a reason, and it's probably not that the reader couldn't see how brilliantly your story shines.

If you must write to the people or organization that rejected you, thank them for their comments and ask if you may submit to them again. They will respect your friendly manner and you may create a worthwhile relationship. I became a reader for, found my manager through, and got help writing this book all with an agency that originally rejected one of my scripts.

Here's how not to respond to rejection. Do not write a scathing letter back arguing your case, insulting the reader or threatening bodily harm (yes, this happens). You will not only be burning a bridge, you'll be ending your career before it starts.

EASY TO FOLLOW INSTRUCTIONS...

WHAT IS THE MAIN CHALLENGE(S) OF THIS CHARACTER?

What is your character after? If he is the protagonist, does he simply want to defeat the antagonist? Does your antagonist want to steal a nuclear weapon? Even minor characters work here. Does the pizza man want to simply deliver the pizza, get his money and go, or is he hoping to catch a glimpse of his crush as she digs through her purse for cash? Knowing the answer to this question for every character is key.

HOW DID THESE CHARACTERS MEET?

Basically the "where, when, who, what and how." If they have a relationship, they had to meet somehow. Explain in detail or as best you can!

WHAT WENT WRONG IN THE RELATIONSHIP?

Even if the two characters you're using are best buddies, everyone hits a bump in the road occasionally. What's the bump? What makes their relationship strong or weak? If you're filling out the form for your protagonist and antagonist the answer should be simple. Why are they on opposite sides of the fence? Were they friends once? Have they always been at odds?

INTERESTS

What do your characters do in their spare time? Hobbies and passions are rarely what people do for work, yet often these interests are what shape their lives.

WHAT IS THE ULTIMATE GOAL OF THIS CHARACTER?

Pretty basic. Does your protagonist want to save or destroy the world? A little dramatic, but this question boils your characters down to the bare bones and highlights the driving force behind their every action and word.

CORE BELIEFS

Often, character traits are defined by your character's beliefs. Some of the most complex characters are the ones breaking their own rules, defying their own beliefs. Belief, or lack thereof, has been the cause of many major events in human history. It is what we are passionate about and sometimes even willing to die for. You will be at the top of your game if you know what your characters are all about.

Screenplay/Project: _____ Date: _____

PROTAGONIST	ANTAGONIST
Name:	Name:
Main challenge(s) for this character?	Main challenge(s) for this character?
How did these characters meet?	
What went wrong/changed in the relationship?	What went wrong/changed in the relationship?
Interests:	Interests:
Ultimate goals of this character?	Ultimate goals of this character?
Core beliefs of this character?	Core beliefs of this character?

CHARACTER RELATIONSHIPS WORKSHEET

Screenplay/Project: _____ Date: _____

PROTAGONIST	ANTAGONIST
Name:	Name:
Main challenge(s) for this character?	Main challenge(s) for this character?

How did these characters meet?

What went wrong/changed in the relationship?	What went wrong/changed in the relationship?
Interests:	Interests:
Ultimate goals of this character?	Ultimate goals of this character?
Core beliefs of this character?	Core beliefs of this character?

CHARACTER RELATIONSHIPS WORKSHEET

Screenplay/Project: _____ Date: _____

PROTAGONIST	ANTAGONIST
Name:	Name:
Main challenge(s) for this character?	Main challenge(s) for this character?
How did these characters meet?	
What went wrong/changed in the relationship?	What went wrong/changed in the relationship?
Interests:	Interests:
Ultimate goals of this character?	Ultimate goals of this character?
Core beliefs of this character?	Core beliefs of this character?

CHARACTER RELATIONSHIPS WORKSHEET

Screenplay/Project: _____   Date: _____

PROTAGONIST	ANTAGONIST
Name:	Name:
Main challenge(s) for this character?	Main challenge(s) for this character?

How did these characters meet?

What went wrong/changed in the relationship?	What went wrong/changed in the relationship?
Interests:	Interests:
Ultimate goals of this character?	Ultimate goals of this character?
Core beliefs of this character?	Core beliefs of this character?

CHARACTER RELATIONSHIPS WORKSHEET

The Screenplay Workbook

Screenplay/Project: _____ Date: _____

PROTAGONIST	ANTAGONIST
Name:	Name:
Main challenge(s) for this character?	Main challenge(s) for this character?

How did these characters meet?

What went wrong/changed in the relationship?	What went wrong/changed in the relationship?
Interests:	Interests:
Ultimate goals of this character?	Ultimate goals of this character?
Core beliefs of this character?	Core beliefs of this character?

CHARACTER RELATIONSHIPS WORKSHEET

Screenplay/Project: _____ Date: _____

PROTAGONIST	ANTAGONIST
Name:	Name:
Main challenge(s) for this character?	Main challenge(s) for this character?

How did these characters meet?

What went wrong/changed in the relationship?	What went wrong/changed in the relationship?
Interests:	Interests:
Ultimate goals of this character?	Ultimate goals of this character?
Core beliefs of this character?	Core beliefs of this character?

CHARACTER RELATIONSHIPS WORKSHEET

Screenplay/Project: _____ Date: _____

PROTAGONIST	ANTAGONIST
Name:	Name:
Main challenge(s) for this character?	Main challenge(s) for this character?
How did these characters meet?	
What went wrong/changed in the relationship?	What went wrong/changed in the relationship?
Interests:	Interests:
Ultimate goals of this character?	Ultimate goals of this character?
Core beliefs of this character?	Core beliefs of this character?

CHARACTER RELATIONSHIPS WORKSHEET

Screenplay/Project: _____ Date: _____

PROTAGONIST	ANTAGONIST
Name:	Name:
Main challenge(s) for this character?	Main challenge(s) for this character?

How did these characters meet?

What went wrong/changed in the relationship?	What went wrong/changed in the relationship?
Interests:	Interests:
Ultimate goals of this character?	Ultimate goals of this character?
Core beliefs of this character?	Core beliefs of this character?

Screenplay/Project: _____ Date: _____

PROTAGONIST	ANTAGONIST
Name:	Name:
Main challenge(s) for this character?	Main challenge(s) for this character?

How did these characters meet?

What went wrong/changed in the relationship?	What went wrong/changed in the relationship?
Interests:	Interests:
Ultimate goals of this character?	Ultimate goals of this character?
Core beliefs of this character?	Core beliefs of this character?

Screenplay/Project: _____ Date: _____

PROTAGONIST	ANTAGONIST
Name:	Name:
Main challenge(s) for this character?	Main challenge(s) for this character?
How did these characters meet?	
What went wrong/changed in the relationship?	What went wrong/changed in the relationship?
Interests:	Interests:
Ultimate goals of this character?	Ultimate goals of this character?
Core beliefs of this character?	Core beliefs of this character?

CHARACTER RELATIONSHIPS WORKSHEET

Screenplay/Project: _____ Date: _____

PROTAGONIST	ANTAGONIST
Name:	Name:
Main challenge(s) for this character?	Main challenge(s) for this character?
How did these characters meet?	
What went wrong/changed in the relationship?	What went wrong/changed in the relationship?
Interests:	Interests:
Ultimate goals of this character?	Ultimate goals of this character?
Core beliefs of this character?	Core beliefs of this character?

Screenplay/Project: _____   Date: _____

PROTAGONIST	ANTAGONIST
Name:	Name:
Main challenge(s) for this character?	Main challenge(s) for this character?

How did these characters meet?

What went wrong/changed in the relationship?	What went wrong/changed in the relationship?
Interests:	Interests:
Ultimate goals of this character?	Ultimate goals of this character?
Core beliefs of this character?	Core beliefs of this character?

CHARACTER RELATIONSHIPS WORKSHEET

Screenplay/Project: _____ Date: _____

PROTAGONIST	ANTAGONIST
Name:	Name:
Main challenge(s) for this character?	Main challenge(s) for this character?

How did these characters meet?

What went wrong/changed in the relationship?	What went wrong/changed in the relationship?
Interests:	Interests:
Ultimate goals of this character?	Ultimate goals of this character?
Core beliefs of this character?	Core beliefs of this character?

 **The Screenplay Workbook** **CHARACTER RELATIONSHIPS WORKSHEET**

Screenplay/Project: _____ Date: _____

PROTAGONIST	ANTAGONIST
Name:	Name:
Main challenge(s) for this character?	Main challenge(s) for this character?

How did these characters meet?

What went wrong/changed in the relationship?	What went wrong/changed in the relationship?
Interests:	Interests:
Ultimate goals of this character?	Ultimate goals of this character?
Core beliefs of this character?	Core beliefs of this character?

CHARACTER RELATIONSHIPS WORKSHEET

Screenplay/Project: _____ Date: _____

PROTAGONIST	ANTAGONIST
Name:	Name:
Main challenge(s) for this character?	Main challenge(s) for this character?
How did these characters meet?	
What went wrong/changed in the relationship?	What went wrong/changed in the relationship?
Interests:	Interests:
Ultimate goals of this character?	Ultimate goals of this character?
Core beliefs of this character?	Core beliefs of this character?

CHARACTER RELATIONSHIPS WORKSHEET

Screenplay/Project: _____   Date: _____

PROTAGONIST	ANTAGONIST
Name:	Name:
Main challenge(s) for this character?	Main challenge(s) for this character?

How did these characters meet?

What went wrong/changed in the relationship?	What went wrong/changed in the relationship?
Interests:	Interests:
Ultimate goals of this character?	Ultimate goals of this character?
Core beliefs of this character?	Core beliefs of this character?

CHARACTER RELATIONSHIPS WORKSHEET

Screenplay/Project: _____ Date: _____

PROTAGONIST	ANTAGONIST
Name:	Name:
Main challenge(s) for this character?	Main challenge(s) for this character?
How did these characters meet?	
What went wrong/changed in the relationship?	What went wrong/changed in the relationship?
Interests:	Interests:
Ultimate goals of this character?	Ultimate goals of this character?
Core beliefs of this character?	Core beliefs of this character?

CHARACTER RELATIONSHIPS WORKSHEET

Screenplay/Project: _____ Date: _____

PROTAGONIST	ANTAGONIST
Name:	Name:
Main challenge(s) for this character?	Main challenge(s) for this character?

How did these characters meet?	

What went wrong/changed in the relationship?	What went wrong/changed in the relationship?
Interests:	Interests:
Ultimate goals of this character?	Ultimate goals of this character?
Core beliefs of this character?	Core beliefs of this character?

CHARACTER RELATIONSHIPS WORKSHEET

Screenplay/Project: _____ Date: _____

PROTAGONIST	ANTAGONIST
Name:	Name:
Main challenge(s) for this character?	Main challenge(s) for this character?
How did these characters meet?	
What went wrong/changed in the relationship?	What went wrong/changed in the relationship?
Interests:	Interests:
Ultimate goals of this character?	Ultimate goals of this character?
Core beliefs of this character?	Core beliefs of this character?

CHARACTER RELATIONSHIPS WORKSHEET

Screenplay/Project: _____ Date: _____

PROTAGONIST	ANTAGONIST
Name:	Name:
Main challenge(s) for this character?	Main challenge(s) for this character?

How did these characters meet?

What went wrong/changed in the relationship?	What went wrong/changed in the relationship?
Interests:	Interests:
Ultimate goals of this character?	Ultimate goals of this character?
Core beliefs of this character?	Core beliefs of this character?

The Screenplay Workbook

CHARACTER RELATIONSHIPS WORKSHEET

Screenplay/Project: _____ Date: _____

PROTAGONIST	ANTAGONIST
Name:	Name:
Main challenge(s) for this character?	Main challenge(s) for this character?

How did these characters meet?

What went wrong/changed in the relationship?	What went wrong/changed in the relationship?
Interests:	Interests:
Ultimate goals of this character?	Ultimate goals of this character?
Core beliefs of this character?	Core beliefs of this character?

 **CHARACTER RELATIONSHIPS WORKSHEET**

Screenplay/Project: _____ Date: _____

PROTAGONIST	ANTAGONIST
Name:	Name:
Main challenge(s) for this character?	Main challenge(s) for this character?
How did these characters meet?	
What went wrong/changed in the relationship?	What went wrong/changed in the relationship?
Interests:	Interests:
Ultimate goals of this character?	Ultimate goals of this character?
Core beliefs of this character?	Core beliefs of this character?

Screenplay/Project: _____ Date: _____

PROTAGONIST	ANTAGONIST
Name:	Name:
Main challenge(s) for this character?	Main challenge(s) for this character?

How did these characters meet?

What went wrong/changed in the relationship?	What went wrong/changed in the relationship?
Interests:	Interests:
Ultimate goals of this character?	Ultimate goals of this character?
Core beliefs of this character?	Core beliefs of this character?

CHARACTER RELATIONSHIPS WORKSHEET

Screenplay/Project: _____ Date: _____

PROTAGONIST	ANTAGONIST
Name:	Name:
Main challenge(s) for this character?	Main challenge(s) for this character?

How did these characters meet?

What went wrong/changed in the relationship?	What went wrong/changed in the relationship?
Interests:	Interests:
Ultimate goals of this character?	Ultimate goals of this character?
Core beliefs of this character?	Core beliefs of this character?

Screenplay/Project: _____ Date: _____

PROTAGONIST	ANTAGONIST
Name:	Name:
Main challenge(s) for this character?	Main challenge(s) for this character?

How did these characters meet?

What went wrong/changed in the relationship?	What went wrong/changed in the relationship?
Interests:	Interests:
Ultimate goals of this character?	Ultimate goals of this character?
Core beliefs of this character?	Core beliefs of this character?

**The computer knew this day would come since
John installed that expensive, "easy to use"
story development software.**

Chapter 5

PLOT STRUCTURE

If your story was a skyscraper, the plot would be its steel frame. It is the key that brings every other literary element together into a seamless structure. And just as every building has a standard structure, a building code so to speak, so does a screenplay. They can be broken down into three very basic units we call Acts. Act I, Act II and Act III are all common language among screenwriters. But what makes up an act? What smaller elements define the movement of an act?

We've broken plot structure down into smaller units found within each act. These structural units are found in screenplays, books and plays. Taken from historical storytelling, these are tried and true story elements; if obeyed, they will enhance your storyline and follow a format that everyone, absolutely everyone, will be able to understand with ease. Here's a brief explanation of how plot structure fits into the traditional three acts.

ACT I: In Act One we find Exposition and Rising Action. This is the beginning of your story and the introduction to what lies ahead. Picture your story as a space shuttle launch. Stage one is ignition; this is *Exposition*. Your story begins with a bang. Stage two; the shuttle is launched into the air, increasing in speed with every second. Your *Rising Action* careens into your first plot point (found on the Plot Point worksheet) causing the spent fuel tanks to drop away and thrust your story into Act II.

ACT II: This act is the center and longest portion of your script. It includes Conflict and Climax. *Conflict* is the inevitable portion of your story where things go wrong and your characters have to face the challenge. Your space shuttle hits turbulence and is knocked off course, threatening to career back to earth. *Climax* is the final showdown between your characters and challenge. This is where the ultimate outcome of your story is decided. Your characters have prepared and make their last effort to correct the shuttle's trajectory. They succeed and the shuttle's course it corrected, safely passing through plot point two.

ACT III: This is the last part of your story. Your first step is *Falling Action*—the crew is safe. The have entered space and can begin repairs. Next is *Resolution*—NASA makes contact, congratulates the crew on a job well done and tells them they're all getting promoted. Lastly, is *Denouement*—This is the end of your story. Tie up all the loose ends and give the audience a peek at what the future holds. The crew declines NASA promotion, as it means desk jobs for everyone and they'd rather risk life and limb again than be stuck in cubicles. They return to Earth to a heroic welcome and their loving families.

For additional clarification on plot structure, see the plot structure instructions page.

Some of you may be saying, "But I'm a writer! I can't conform to structure, rules, the norm! This stuff will butcher my story!"

Now, if you've managed to successfully write and sell a masterpiece that breaks the rules and rewrites thousands of years of storytelling structure—hey, bravo, good for you! But chances are, you have yet to sell that first screenplay, and now is the time to wake up, face reality and calm down. On the contrary, if you are a professional writer, you probably have no complaints about structure. There is an infinite amount of room to stretch your imagination within the boundaries of plot structure.

Feel free to expand and shrink down areas of the plot structure. Nothing is concrete. Experiment. Plot structure is a mere plumb line to help keep you on the straight and narrow. Veer too far from the path and you may not find your way back. Can you imagine a movie with no climax, no resolution? Not every skyscraper is the same, but every architect must consider gravity, wind and aesthetics—and no one can live or work in an unfinished construction site.

JEREMY'S INSIDE SCOOP

Speeling ain't evarything know you. Was that sentence distracting? Good. Now don't do that in a script. Okay, feel free to do it in your first draft. At that point, your story is more important than your spelling or grammar skills. But do not send your first draft out—ever. Spell check and grammar check everything. And don't just trust your computer's spell check. Give your script to two people whose literary skills you trust and have them check it for spelling, typos, etc. (I use my wife and my manager.) Then check it again yourself. After this lengthy process you'll still probably have one or two mistakes, but at least they shouldn't be glaring.

You don't want your screenplay to read like English is your second language. It's distracting; it's unprofessional; it's often downright funny. I've read scenes that were meant to be tearjerking or horrific and laughed all the way through because the spelling and grammar were so bad. If you get a reader to laugh, you want it to be because what you've written is funny, not because your writing skills are laughable.

EASY TO FOLLOW INSTRUCTIONS...

1. EXPOSITION (BEGINNING)

Exposition is a precursor to the actual story. This is often seen in what is called the "hook." A snippet of intriguing information that pulls us into the story. Perhaps we see a traumatic event from the characters childhood, or the antagonist killing someone. Whatever the case, it sets up the rest of the story.

2. RISING ACTION

This is when a challenge enters the story. The main character is faced with a challenge that must be met or an antagonist who must be defeated. This point of the story is very similar to Step 2 of the Character Arc Worksheet, but also includes Steps 3-5.

3. CONFLICT

The main character and the challenge (or antagonist) are facing off. They are hunting each other, running from each other and learning the other's weakness, passions and agendas. This is a time of testing, of building tension and preparation.

4. CLIMAX

This is the pinnacle of the story. The action should be most tense. Emotions should be running high (from characters and audience alike). Everything is on the line and we should feel it.

5. FALLING ACTION

The climax is over. Things are winding down. The end is in sight and we're starting to see how the complex threads of the story are coming together.

6. RESOLUTION

The challenge has been met, and beaten. The antagonist has been defeated. The problems of the rising action have been solved.

7. DENOUEMENT (ENDING)

What now? Your characters have succeeded or failed. Do they continue on? Live happily ever after? What happens to them now that the biggest challenge of their life is over? This wraps of the story and gives the audience a sense of closure.

Screenplay/Project: _____   Date: _____

| ACT 1 | ACT 2 | ACT 3 |

plot point 1

plot point 2

page 20-30

page 80-90

1 2 3 4 5 6 7

Write a sentence or two describing the overall action for that segment of your story.

1. Exposition (Beginning):	
2. Rising Action:	
3. Conflict:	
4. Climax:	
5. Falling Action:	
6. Resolution:	
7. Denouement (Ending):	

PLOT STRUCTURE WORKSHEET

Screenplay/Project: _____ Date: _____

ACT 1   ACT 2   ACT 3

plot point 1

plot point 2

page 20-30

page 80-90

Write a sentence or two describing the overall action for that segment of your story.

1. Exposition (Beginning):	
2. Rising Action:	
3. Conflict:	
4. Climax:	
5. Falling Action:	
6. Resolution:	
7. Denouement (Ending):	

PLOT STRUCTURE WORKSHEET

Screenplay/Project: _____ Date: _____

| ACT 1 | ACT 2 | ACT 3 |

plot point 1 — page 20-30

plot point 2 — page 80-90

Write a sentence or two describing the overall action for that segment of your story.

1. Exposition (Beginning):	
2. Rising Action:	
3. Conflict:	
4. Climax:	
5. Falling Action:	
6. Resolution:	
7. Denouement (Ending):	

PLOT STRUCTURE WORKSHEET

Screenplay/Project: _____   Date: _____

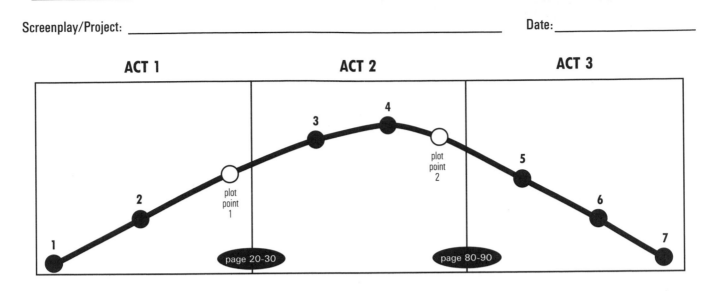

ACT 1   **ACT 2**   **ACT 3**

3   4

plot point 1

2

1   page 20-30

plot point 2

5

6

7

page 80-90

Write a sentence or two describing the overall action for that segment of your story.

1. Exposition (Beginning):	
2. Rising Action:	
3. Conflict:	
4. Climax:	
5. Falling Action:	
6. Resolution:	
7. Denouement (Ending):	

Screenplay/Project: _____ Date: _____

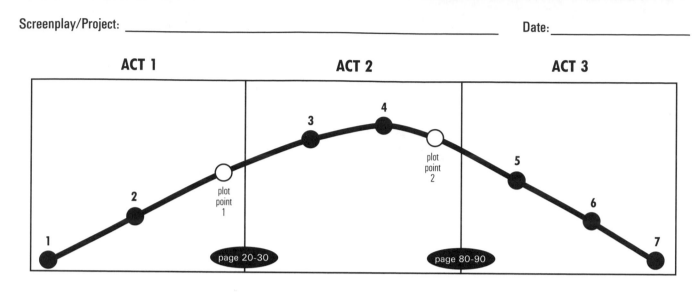

Write a sentence or two describing the overall action for that segment of your story.

1. Exposition (Beginning):	
2. Rising Action:	
3. Conflict:	
4. Climax:	
5. Falling Action:	
6. Resolution:	
7. Denouement (Ending):	

While humorous, pin the tail on the plot point should be reserved for weekend night writers' groups, not for actually writing.

Chapter 6
PLOT POINTS

Plot Points are an integral part of screenwriting made up of Plot Point 1, a turning point and Plot Point 2.... All right, now what's this, you ask? We already have plot structure; what's the deal with plot points? What the heck is the difference between them and why should I even bother with plot points? There are only two of them and what's with the "turning point?" Is this some kind of defunct plot point?

If you didn't ask any of these questions, pretend you did—you'll thank us later!

Plot points are vital to successful screenplays. They are the main events that shape your story and push it ever onward towards the conclusion. They are specifically important in screenplays and often fall between certain page numbers. Screenplays are like well-choreographed musicals. Every beat is timed to land with a footfall. Every crescendo of music emulates a rise and fall in action. Plot points are one of the elements that help screenwriters never miss a beat. Just as a conductor waves his baton in three beats, so the screenwriter writes his screenplay.

"But my screenplay is 150 pages long! I couldn't possibly have Plot Point 2 by page ninety! These plot points are a sham!"

If, in fact, your spec screenplay is over 120 pages (assuming you haven't been hired to write the next *Titanic*) you need to trim the page count way down. No joke. No way around it. Grit your teeth and start deleting until your screenplay reaches 120 pages and at least gets close to fitting the plot point page numbers.

You can choose to ignore this rule of screenwriting, but be warned that if you do, every producer in Hollywood will ignore your script just as quickly.

"But why?" you might ask. Because Hollywood is a money-making machine. Screenplays usually work out to be a page per minute when put on film. So a 120-page screenplay takes up two hours of time at the theater. Add a half hour for clean up and refilling of the seats and you can show a movie every two and a half hours. Theaters show movies from about 11:00 a.m. to 1 a.m., roughly fourteen hours. 14 / 2.5 = 5.6. So a theater can show roughly six movies on a single screen per day (not all movies are exactly 2 hours long, most are less.) But now add thirty pages to your screenplay, then thirty minutes to you film time and redo the math. 14 / 3 = 4.6. You've lost one showing per screen, per day—and that can add up to millions. Unless you're a powerhouse like James Cameron or Ron Howard, keep the page count to 120. It's going to help you make a sale and help your film make more money at the box office.

JEREMY'S INSIDE SCOOP

Think you're tricky? Think no one will notice how you oh-so-cleverly tweaked your 160 page screenplay into a 120-page masterpiece? Think again. Here are a few ways screenwriters try to "trim" their screenplay down to 120 pages that you should never do:

1. Using 10-point fonts – Readers are used to seeing 12-point font. They'll know the font size is too small with just a glance.

2. Increasing margins (top, bottom and sides) – Your page will look crowded. Readers like to see lots of white space on a page, it reflects the writer's knowledge of less is more.

3. Compressing text into massive descriptive paragraphs – You're writing a screenplay, not a novel. Only write what you need, cut everything else.

You may think no one will notice, but these tricks make your script stand out from the rest, in the worst way possible.

There is no way to trim a too-long a screenplay to 120 pages without deleting text. If you go over 120 pages, you've probably said too much and a more concise screenplay is likely be more powerful anyway. Make the Backspace/Delete key your friend. You won't regret it. A large part of writing is knowing what to delete.

EASY TO FOLLOW INSTRUCTIONS...

PLOT POINT 1 (PAGES 20-30):

Plot Point 1 thrusts your story from the first to second act. Your character comes to the realization that a challenge exists and he commits to meeting it, sending him on a straight path toward a goal.

TURNING POINT (PAGES 55-65):

The Turning Point is a bend in the road. Circumstances change and the original goal of your character is altered slightly or completely. Characters who were running away from danger may now decide to run towards it. This new goal can replace, work in tandem with, or take precedence over the first goal.

PLOT POINT 2 (PAGES 80-90):

Plot Point 2 moves your story from the second to third act. It is usually a monumental event that often coincides with the story's climax. Your character has almost reached the end of the road, but it's downhill from here. This is the catalyst for the events that will lead to the resolution of your story.

PLOT POINTS WORKSHEET

Screenplay/Project: _____   Date: _____

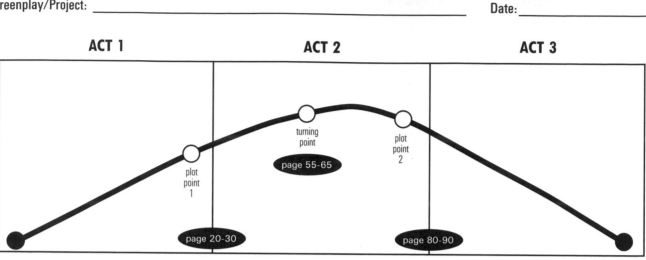

ACT 1   ACT 2   ACT 3

turning
point

page 55-65

plot
point
2

plot
point
1

page 20-30   page 80-90

**In each space write a brief description of the event,
and how it pushes your story forward and in a new direction**

Plot Point 1 (pages 20-30)	
Turning Point (pages 55-65)	
Plot Point 2 (pages 80-90)	

Screenplay/Project: _____   Date: _____

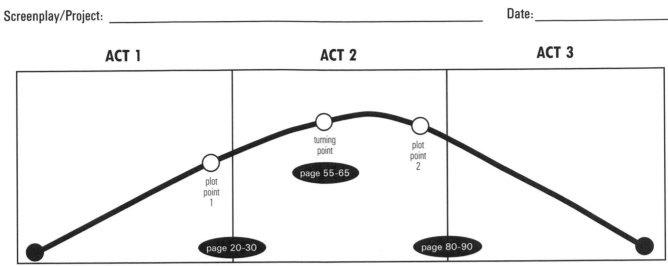

ACT 1   ACT 2   ACT 3

plot point 1

turning point
page 55-65

plot point 2

page 20-30

page 80-90

**In each space write a brief description of the event,
and how it pushes your story forward and in a new direction**

Plot Point 1 (pages 20-30)	
Turning Point (pages 55-65)	
Plot Point 2 (pages 80-90)	

PLOT POINTS WORKSHEET

Screenplay/Project: _____   Date: _____

| | ACT 1 | ACT 2 | ACT 3 |

ACT 1   **ACT 2**   **ACT 3**

plot point 1 — page 20-30

turning point — page 55-65

plot point 2 — page 80-90

**In each space write a brief description of the event,
and how it pushes your story forward and in a new direction**

Plot Point 1 (pages 20-30)	
Turning Point (pages 55-65)	
Plot Point 2 (pages 80-90)	

Screenplay/Project: _____   Date: _____

ACT 1   **ACT 2**   **ACT 3**

plot point 1

turning point
page 55-65

plot point 2

page 20-30

page 80-90

**In each space write a brief description of the event,
and how it pushes your story forward and in a new direction**

Plot Point 1 (pages 20-30)	
Turning Point (pages 55-65)	
Plot Point 2 (pages 80-90)	

PLOT POINTS WORKSHEET

Screenplay/Project: _____ Date: _____

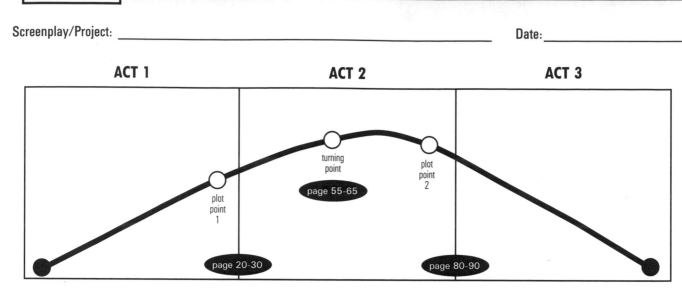

**In each space write a brief description of the event,
and how it pushes your story forward and in a new direction**

Plot Point 1 (pages 20-30)	
Turning Point (pages 55-65)	
Plot Point 2 (pages 80-90)	

**After hours of writing, John felt as flat
as his characters.**

Chapter 7

CHARACTER ARC

What is character arc? What is it good for? And why the heck should I bother filling out a work-sheet for character arc when I could be writing the first pages of my masterpiece-gonna-make-me-a-millionaire-blockbuster screenplay?

All reasonable questions, and all easily answered. Character arc is an important element found in any well-developed character. And without well-developed characters, how can your story ever hope to be a masterpiece? A character arc is a chart of the character's growth (or lack of growth) on an emotional and physical level throughout the storyline of your screenplay. A good screenplay takes advantage of character arc and draws the audience into the story. We see the character's faults, fears, passions and then watch as these traits expand, get destroyed or remain unchanged. Even if your story is a high-tech, sci-fi, action script—if the characters are stagnant, your masterpiece will end up being used for a late afternoon round of trashcan hoops.

A character arc is a blueprint for character development. This development usually coincides with the story's progression. Once finished with your Character Arc worksheet, compare it with your completed Plot Point worksheet and see if they match up. Do turning points in your characters' development match turning points in the screenplay's storyline?

Imagine how dull the battle between Luke and Darth Vader would have been if Luke weren't also dealing with the news that Vader was his father. Physical and emotional elements can have an impact while separate, but together, they are a powerful team. To further illustrate the importance of combining emotional story elements with physical story elements, we have separated the two on the worksheet. This allows the writer to view how the physical world is affecting the emotional world, and vice versa.

Most writers break down character arc into twelve steps, as we have done on the worksheet. The language for these steps varies, depending on each writer's personal preference. We prefer to lay out a character's development using a series of problems or challenges that the character faces and uses to grow.

Now that you understand why character arc is not only a good writing tool, but a necessary one, read the following instructions and see what each step means, and how they apply to your character and overall storyline.

JEREMY'S INSIDE SCOOP

Read screenplays. It sounds dumb and obvious, but it is very easy to pick out a writer who has never looked at another screenplay. You can purchase screenplays at bookstores, through online booksellers and can download them for free from websites like Drew's Script-O-Rama (www.script-o-rama.com.) Get copies of your favorite films and read them like books. Your writing will improve. Your sense of style and timing will be honed. You'll learn what a professional screenplay looks (and reads) like and will be able to apply that knowledge to your own writing.

EASY TO FOLLOW INSTRUCTIONS...

For the following instructions we are going to use two imaginary characters to illustrate each step in two very different stories. Their names: Bob and Bill.

STEP 1. NORMAL LIFE (WITHOUT CHALLENGE)

This is your character living a normal life. Let's say that Bob has a perfect life, happy in every way. He's an average, present-day, working man with a cute girlfriend named Sally. But poor Bill has an awful life, full of turmoil. He's a knight in the middle ages, where every day is a struggle to survive. The important point with each character is that it is their normal lives—not the most exciting or challenging part of their lives—that is what your story should be about!

STEP 2. INTRODUCED TO CHALLENGE

This is the first time your character gets wind of the problem/challenge. They could be told about it, see it, hear it or have a direct confrontation with it. Whatever the case, your character now knows (or has an inkling) that the problem/challenge exists. In this case, Bob hears at the water cooler that Sally is thinking about leaving him, while Bill hears about a dragon that is been destroying distant villages.

STEP 3. DENIAL OF CHALLENGE

Your character may avoid, deny the existence of, or overlook the challenge. In all scenarios they are resistant to the idea of facing the challenge. Bob certainly doesn't believe that his darling Sally could ever be dissatisfied with their relationship, and Bill...well, Bill doesn't believe in dragons. The overall theme here is that the character doesn't welcome what they know of the challenge.

STEP 4. FIRST ACKNOWLEDGEMENT OF THE CHALLENGE

The opposite of step three. The challenge can't be denied, ignored or overlooked any longer. The character admits that the challenge exists. Bob takes a closer look at his relationship and finds a void. Bill sees the dragon from a distance and finally believes it's real.

STEP 5. COMMITMENT TO FACE THE CHALLENGE*

After acknowledging the existence of the challenge, the character now accepts the challenge. Bob doesn't want to lose Sally and commits to filling the void in their relationship. Bill signs up with the local wizard to take dragon-slaying lessons.

*Step 5 coincides with the first plot point of a screenplay, between pages 20 and 30. The event that thrusts your story into the second act is often the same event that thrusts your character into a new level of development. The character decides to face the challenge, thus moving the story forward.

STEP 6. FEELING OUT THE CHALLENGE

This is the step that will take up the largest amount of time to explore in your story. It could be made up of several smaller challenges, lessons or insights, all leading your character to a point in their personal growth where they begin to feel ready to tackle the main challenge.

Bob faces an ex-girlfriend and finds his failure to commit was the root of their problems, while at the same time attempts to not get neurotic about Sally meeting up with her ex-boyfriend. Bill, on the other hand, picks up a few magic tricks, kills an ogre, befriends a magical horse with the ability to run at super speed and falls in love with the fair maiden who's scheduled to be eaten by the dragon the next time its voracious appetite is to be appeased. Still following? Good.

STEP 7. PREPARING FOR THE ULTIMATE CHALLENGE

The point here is that they feel ready (whether they are or not is a different story) to tackle their challenges and are preparing to do so. Bill stands outside the dragon's cave, while Bob is in the bathroom, preparing to pop the question to Sally. They are both on the brink.

STEP 8. FIRST ATTEMPT

This is where your character makes the leap to direct confrontation. They see the solution and they go for it. Sword in hand and protected by a magical spell, Bill charges in to face the dragon.

Bob, still sweating it out in front of the mirror, sucks up his fears, barges out of the bathroom and pops the question to an awaiting Sally. This is the big push for what your character (falsely) believes is the finish line.

STEP 9. RESULTS OF FIRST ATTEMPT (STEP 8)

Bill runs into the cave and faces the dragon. Only the dragon is ready, the size of a house and can breathe fire. What are the results?

What about Bob? Does Sally say, "Yes!" or "No!"? Was the first attempt at facing the challenge a success? If yes, what's left to do? Why isn't the story over? Is there more to the challenge then first realized? Does you character fail miserably? How does this defeat leave your character's emotional state? This is the aftermath, good or bad, for your character's first attempt. Some people call this the "all is lost" moment; when it seems that, no matter what, the challenge can't be beat.

STEP 10. SECOND ACKNOWLEDGEMENT OF CHALLENGE**

Okay, so the dragon isn't dead and Sally says no. What now? Do Bob and Bill just walk away? Give up? The End? Unlikely. That wouldn't make a very good story. So, what then? This is the point where the character realizes that the first attempt either failed miserably or at least fell short.

**This step also coincides with the second plot point, thrusting the story into the third act and your character into the final leg of his or her development.

STEP 11. FACING THE FINAL CHALLENGE

This is the last chance for your character to face the challenge. Will they run or fight? Bill returns to the cave, better prepared, and more determined then ever, having emotionally reined in the fear, doubt or other emotional baggage that worked against him before. Bob comes to the final realization that Sally doesn't define his life. He can face her one last time because the result, good or bad, doesn't scare him anymore.

STEP 12. DEFEATING THE FINAL CHALLENGE

Your character faces the challenge one final time. Does your character fail again, and for good? Does your character save the day and get the girl? What is the outcome of this final challenge? What final emotional victory or defeat is achieved? Does Bill slay the dragon, thus saving the villagers; or does he die, teaching the lesson that dragons shouldn't be messed with? Does Bob win Sally back or does she leave him for good?

THIS IS THE END OF YOUR STORY. The full realization and results of your character's growth should be crystal clear.

Screenplay/Project: _____ Date: _____

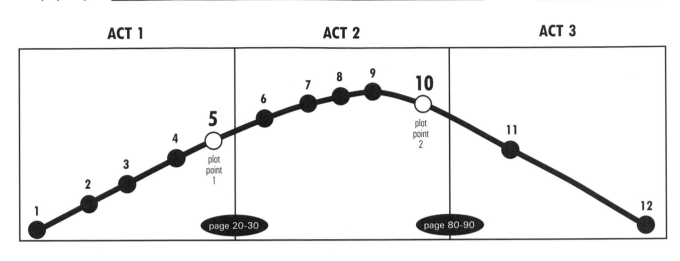

Character Name: _____ ☐ Main ☐ Supporting

	PHYSICAL	EMOTIONAL
1. Normal life (without challenge):		
2. Introduced to challenge:		
3. Denial of challenge:		
4. First acknowledgment of challenge:		
5. Commitment to face challenge:		
6. Feeling out challenge:		
7. Preparing for ultimate challenge:		
8. First attempt:		
9. Results of first attempt:		
10. Second acknowledgment of challenge:		
11. Face final challenge:		
12. Defeating final challenge:		

Screenplay/Project: _____ Date: _____

ACT 1	ACT 2	ACT 3

plot point 1
page 20-30

plot point 2
page 80-90

Character Name: _____ ☐ Main ☐ Supporting

	PHYSICAL	EMOTIONAL
1. Normal life (without challenge):		
2. Introduced to challenge:		
3. Denial of challenge:		
4. First acknowledgment of challenge:		
5. Commitment to face challenge:		
6. Feeling out challenge:		
7. Preparing for ultimate challenge:		
8. First attempt:		
9. Results of first attempt:		
10. Second acknowledgment of challenge:		
11. Face final challenge:		
12. Defeating final challenge:		

Screenplay/Project: _____   Date: _____

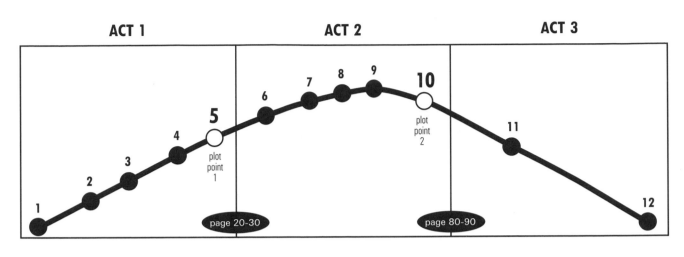

ACT 1   **ACT 2**   **ACT 3**

Character Name: _____   ☐ Main   ☐ Supporting

	PHYSICAL	EMOTIONAL
1. Normal life (without challenge):		
2. Introduced to challenge:		
3. Denial of challenge:		
4. First acknowledgment of challenge:		
5. Commitment to face challenge:		
6. Feeling out challenge:		
7. Preparing for ultimate challenge:		
8. First attempt:		
9. Results of first attempt:		
10. Second acknowledgment of challenge:		
11. Face final challenge:		
12. Defeating final challenge:		

CHARACTER ARC WORKSHEET

Screenplay/Project: _____   Date: _____

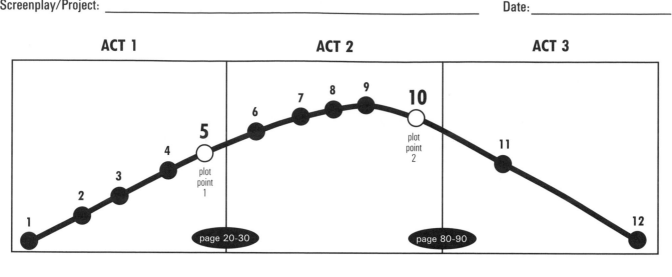

ACT 1   **ACT 2**   **ACT 3**

plot point 1 — page 20-30

plot point 2 — page 80-90

Character Name: _____   ☐ Main ☐ Supporting

	PHYSICAL	EMOTIONAL
1. Normal life (without challenge):		
2. Introduced to challenge:		
3. Denial of challenge:		
4. First acknowledgment of challenge:		
5. Commitment to face challenge:		
6. Feeling out challenge:		
7. Preparing for ultimate challenge:		
8. First attempt:		
9. Results of first attempt:		
10. Second acknowledgment of challenge:		
11. Face final challenge:		
12. Defeating final challenge:		

CHARACTER ARC WORKSHEET

Screenplay/Project: _____   Date: _____

ACT 1	ACT 2	ACT 3

Character Name: _____   ☐ Main   ☐ Supporting

	PHYSICAL	EMOTIONAL
1. Normal life (without challenge):		
2. Introduced to challenge:		
3. Denial of challenge:		
4. First acknowledgment of challenge:		
5. Commitment to face challenge:		
6. Feeling out challenge:		
7. Preparing for ultimate challenge:		
8. First attempt:		
9. Results of first attempt:		
10. Second acknowledgment of challenge:		
11. Face final challenge:		
12. Defeating final challenge:		

CHARACTER ARC WORKSHEET

Screenplay/Project: _____   Date: _____

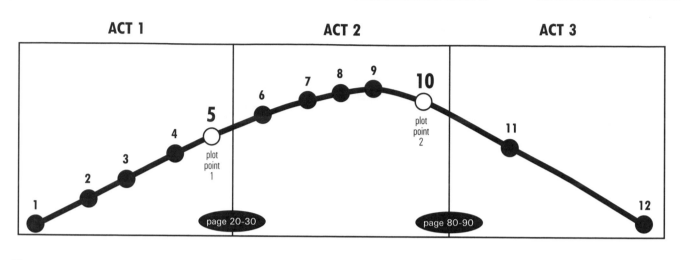

ACT 1   ACT 2   ACT 3

page 20-30   page 80-90

Character Name: _____   ☐ Main   ☐ Supporting

	PHYSICAL	EMOTIONAL
1. Normal life (without challenge):		
2. Introduced to challenge:		
3. Denial of challenge:		
4. First acknowledgment of challenge:		
5. Commitment to face challenge:		
6. Feeling out challenge:		
7. Preparing for ultimate challenge:		
8. First attempt:		
9. Results of first attempt:		
10. Second acknowledgment of challenge:		
11. Face final challenge:		
12. Defeating final challenge:		

Screenplay/Project: _____ Date: _____

ACT 1	ACT 2	ACT 3

Character Name: _____ ☐ Main ☐ Supporting

	PHYSICAL	**EMOTIONAL**
1. Normal life (without challenge):		
2. Introduced to challenge:		
3. Denial of challenge:		
4. First acknowledgment of challenge:		
5. Commitment to face challenge:		
6. Feeling out challenge:		
7. Preparing for ultimate challenge:		
8. First attempt:		
9. Results of first attempt:		
10. Second acknowledgment of challenge:		
11. Face final challenge:		
12. Defeating final challenge:		

CHARACTER ARC WORKSHEET

Screenplay/Project: _____   Date: _____

ACT 1 **ACT 2** **ACT 3**

1 2 3 4 **5** plot point 1 6 7 8 9 **10** plot point 2 11 12

page 20-30 page 80-90

Character Name: _____ ☐ Main ☐ Supporting

	PHYSICAL	EMOTIONAL
1. Normal life (without challenge):		
2. Introduced to challenge:		
3. Denial of challenge:		
4. First acknowledgment of challenge:		
5. Commitment to face challenge:		
6. Feeling out challenge:		
7. Preparing for ultimate challenge:		
8. First attempt:		
9. Results of first attempt:		
10. Second acknowledgment of challenge:		
11. Face final challenge:		
12. Defeating final challenge:		

Screenplay/Project: _____ Date: _____

ACT 1	ACT 2	ACT 3

page 20-30   page 80-90

Character Name: _____ ☐ Main ☐ Supporting

	PHYSICAL	EMOTIONAL
1. Normal life (without challenge):		
2. Introduced to challenge:		
3. Denial of challenge:		
4. First acknowledgment of challenge:		
5. Commitment to face challenge:		
6. Feeling out challenge:		
7. Preparing for ultimate challenge:		
8. First attempt:		
9. Results of first attempt:		
10. Second acknowledgment of challenge:		
11. Face final challenge:		
12. Defeating final challenge:		

CHARACTER ARC WORKSHEET

Screenplay/Project: _____   Date: _____

| ACT 1 | ACT 2 | ACT 3 |

Character Name: _____   ☐ Main   ☐ Supporting

	PHYSICAL	EMOTIONAL
1. Normal life (without challenge):		
2. Introduced to challenge:		
3. Denial of challenge:		
4. First acknowledgment of challenge:		
5. Commitment to face challenge:		
6. Feeling out challenge:		
7. Preparing for ultimate challenge:		
8. First attempt:		
9. Results of first attempt:		
10. Second acknowledgment of challenge:		
11. Face final challenge:		
12. Defeating final challenge:		

CHARACTER ARC WORKSHEET

Screenplay/Project: _____   Date: _____

ACT 1	ACT 2	ACT 3

page 20-30

page 80-90

Character Name: _____   ☐ Main   ☐ Supporting

	PHYSICAL	EMOTIONAL
1. Normal life (without challenge):		
2. Introduced to challenge:		
3. Denial of challenge:		
4. First acknowledgment of challenge:		
5. Commitment to face challenge:		
6. Feeling out challenge:		
7. Preparing for ultimate challenge:		
8. First attempt:		
9. Results of first attempt:		
10. Second acknowledgment of challenge:		
11. Face final challenge:		
12. Defeating final challenge:		

Screenplay/Project: _____   Date: _____

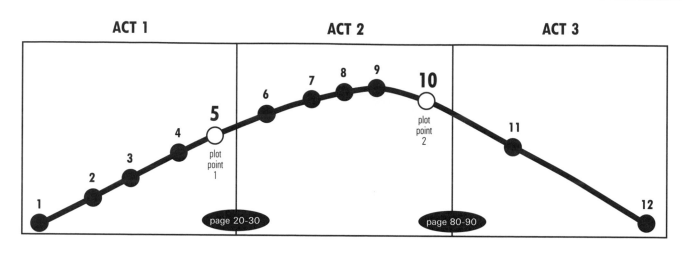

ACT 1   ACT 2   ACT 3

plot point 1 — page 20-30

plot point 2 — page 80-90

Character Name: _____   ☐ Main   ☐ Supporting

	PHYSICAL	EMOTIONAL
1. Normal life (without challenge):		
2. Introduced to challenge:		
3. Denial of challenge:		
4. First acknowledgment of challenge:		
5. Commitment to face challenge:		
6. Feeling out challenge:		
7. Preparing for ultimate challenge:		
8. First attempt:		
9. Results of first attempt:		
10. Second acknowledgment of challenge:		
11. Face final challenge:		
12. Defeating final challenge:		

CHARACTER ARC WORKSHEET

Screenplay/Project: _____ Date: _____

ACT 1	ACT 2	ACT 3

ACT 1 — 1, 2, 3, 4, 5 plot point 1 — page 20-30

ACT 2 — 6, 7, 8, 9, 10 plot point 2 — page 80-90

ACT 3 — 11, 12

Character Name: _____ ☐ Main   ☐ Supporting

	PHYSICAL	EMOTIONAL
1. Normal life (without challenge):		
2. Introduced to challenge:		
3. Denial of challenge:		
4. First acknowledgment of challenge:		
5. Commitment to face challenge:		
6. Feeling out challenge:		
7. Preparing for ultimate challenge:		
8. First attempt:		
9. Results of first attempt:		
10. Second acknowledgment of challenge:		
11. Face final challenge:		
12. Defeating final challenge:		

The Screenplay Workbook

Screenplay/Project: _____ Date: _____

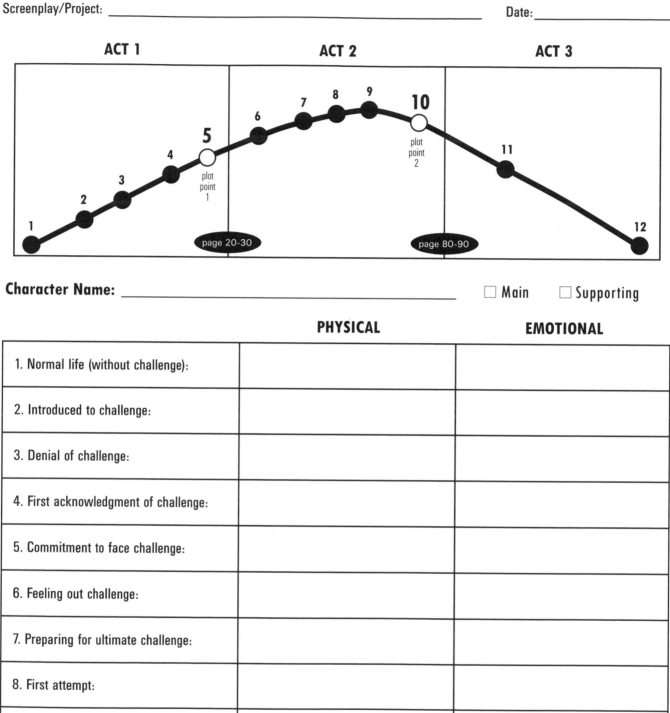

ACT 1   ACT 2   ACT 3

1

2

3

4

5
plot point 1
page 20-30

6

7

8

9

10
plot point 2
page 80-90

11

12

Character Name: _____ ☐ Main ☐ Supporting

	PHYSICAL	EMOTIONAL
1. Normal life (without challenge):		
2. Introduced to challenge:		
3. Denial of challenge:		
4. First acknowledgment of challenge:		
5. Commitment to face challenge:		
6. Feeling out challenge:		
7. Preparing for ultimate challenge:		
8. First attempt:		
9. Results of first attempt:		
10. Second acknowledgment of challenge:		
11. Face final challenge:		
12. Defeating final challenge:		

CHARACTER ARC WORKSHEET

Screenplay/Project: _____ Date: _____

ACT 1   **ACT 2**   **ACT 3**

Character Name: _____ ☐ Main ☐ Supporting

	PHYSICAL	EMOTIONAL
1. Normal life (without challenge):		
2. Introduced to challenge:		
3. Denial of challenge:		
4. First acknowledgment of challenge:		
5. Commitment to face challenge:		
6. Feeling out challenge:		
7. Preparing for ultimate challenge:		
8. First attempt:		
9. Results of first attempt:		
10. Second acknowledgment of challenge:		
11. Face final challenge:		
12. Defeating final challenge:		

Screenplay/Project: _____   Date: _____

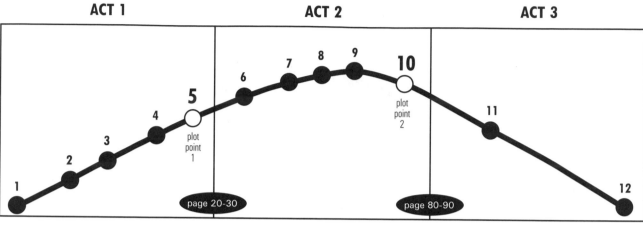

ACT 1   ACT 2   ACT 3

page 20-30   page 80-90

Character Name: _____   ☐ Main   ☐ Supporting

	PHYSICAL	EMOTIONAL
1. Normal life (without challenge):		
2. Introduced to challenge:		
3. Denial of challenge:		
4. First acknowledgment of challenge:		
5. Commitment to face challenge:		
6. Feeling out challenge:		
7. Preparing for ultimate challenge:		
8. First attempt:		
9. Results of first attempt:		
10. Second acknowledgment of challenge:		
11. Face final challenge:		
12. Defeating final challenge:		

CHARACTER ARC WORKSHEET

Screenplay/Project: _____   Date: _____

ACT 1	ACT 2	ACT 3

1

2

3

4

5
plot point 1

page 20-30

6

7

8

9

10
plot point 2

page 80-90

11

12

Character Name: _____   ☐ Main   ☐ Supporting

	PHYSICAL	EMOTIONAL
1. Normal life (without challenge):		
2. Introduced to challenge:		
3. Denial of challenge:		
4. First acknowledgment of challenge:		
5. Commitment to face challenge:		
6. Feeling out challenge:		
7. Preparing for ultimate challenge:		
8. First attempt:		
9. Results of first attempt:		
10. Second acknowledgment of challenge:		
11. Face final challenge:		
12. Defeating final challenge:		

Screenplay/Project: _____   Date: _____

ACT 1	ACT 2	ACT 3

Character Name: _____   ☐ Main   ☐ Supporting

	PHYSICAL	EMOTIONAL
1. Normal life (without challenge):		
2. Introduced to challenge:		
3. Denial of challenge:		
4. First acknowledgment of challenge:		
5. Commitment to face challenge:		
6. Feeling out challenge:		
7. Preparing for ultimate challenge:		
8. First attempt:		
9. Results of first attempt:		
10. Second acknowledgment of challenge:		
11. Face final challenge:		
12. Defeating final challenge:		

Screenplay/Project: _____   Date: _____

ACT 1   **ACT 2**   **ACT 3**

page 20-30   page 80-90

Character Name: _____   ☐ Main   ☐ Supporting

	PHYSICAL	EMOTIONAL
1. Normal life (without challenge):		
2. Introduced to challenge:		
3. Denial of challenge:		
4. First acknowledgment of challenge:		
5. Commitment to face challenge:		
6. Feeling out challenge:		
7. Preparing for ultimate challenge:		
8. First attempt:		
9. Results of first attempt:		
10. Second acknowledgment of challenge:		
11. Face final challenge:		
12. Defeating final challenge:		

The Screenplay Workbook — CHARACTER ARC WORKSHEET

Screenplay/Project: _____ Date: _____

ACT 1   **ACT 2**   **ACT 3**

Character Name: _____ ☐ Main ☐ Supporting

	PHYSICAL	EMOTIONAL
1. Normal life (without challenge):		
2. Introduced to challenge:		
3. Denial of challenge:		
4. First acknowledgment of challenge:		
5. Commitment to face challenge:		
6. Feeling out challenge:		
7. Preparing for ultimate challenge:		
8. First attempt:		
9. Results of first attempt:		
10. Second acknowledgment of challenge:		
11. Face final challenge:		
12. Defeating final challenge:		

Screenplay/Project: _____ Date: _____

ACT 1   **ACT 2**   **ACT 3**

page 20-30   page 80-90

plot point 1 (5)   plot point 2 (10)

1 2 3 4 5 6 7 8 9 10 11 12

Character Name: _____ ☐ Main ☐ Supporting

	PHYSICAL	EMOTIONAL
1. Normal life (without challenge):		
2. Introduced to challenge:		
3. Denial of challenge:		
4. First acknowledgment of challenge:		
5. Commitment to face challenge:		
6. Feeling out challenge:		
7. Preparing for ultimate challenge:		
8. First attempt:		
9. Results of first attempt:		
10. Second acknowledgment of challenge:		
11. Face final challenge:		
12. Defeating final challenge:		

The Screenplay Workbook

CHARACTER ARC WORKSHEET

Screenplay/Project: ____________________ Date: __________

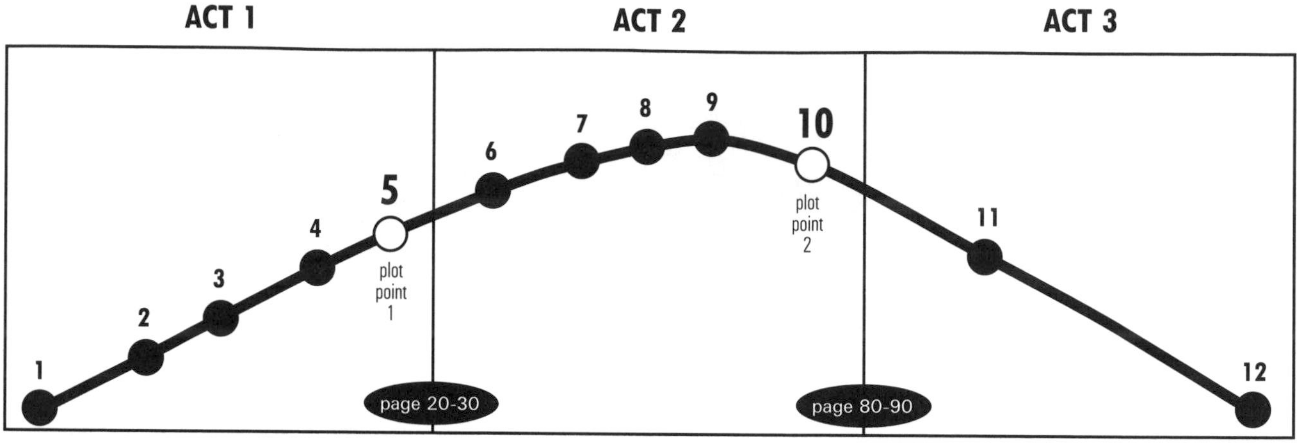
ACT 1
ACT 2
ACT 3
1
2
3
4
5
plot point 1
6
7
8
9
10
plot point 2
11
12
page 20-30
page 80-90

Character Name: ____________________ ☐ Main ☐ Supporting

	PHYSICAL	EMOTIONAL
1. Normal life (without challenge):		
2. Introduced to challenge:		
3. Denial of challenge:		
4. First acknowledgment of challenge:		
5. Commitment to face challenge:		
6. Feeling out challenge:		
7. Preparing for ultimate challenge:		
8. First attempt:		
9. Results of first attempt:		
10. Second acknowledgment of challenge:		
11. Face final challenge:		
12. Defeating final challenge:		

The Screenplay Workbook — CHARACTER ARC WORKSHEET

Screenplay/Project: _____ Date: _____

ACT 1   ACT 2   ACT 3

page 20-30

page 80-90

Character Name: _____ ☐ Main ☐ Supporting

	PHYSICAL	EMOTIONAL
1. Normal life (without challenge):		
2. Introduced to challenge:		
3. Denial of challenge:		
4. First acknowledgment of challenge:		
5. Commitment to face challenge:		
6. Feeling out challenge:		
7. Preparing for ultimate challenge:		
8. First attempt:		
9. Results of first attempt:		
10. Second acknowledgment of challenge:		
11. Face final challenge:		
12. Defeating final challenge:		

CHARACTER ARC WORKSHEET

The Screenplay Workbook

Screenplay/Project: _____ Date: _____

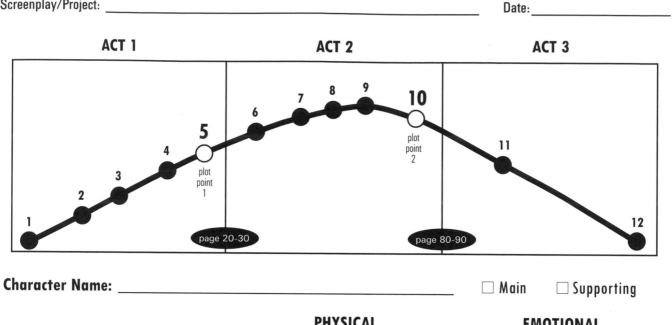

ACT 1   **ACT 2**   **ACT 3**

page 20-30   page 80-90

Character Name: _____ ☐ Main   ☐ Supporting

	PHYSICAL	EMOTIONAL
1. Normal life (without challenge):		
2. Introduced to challenge:		
3. Denial of challenge:		
4. First acknowledgment of challenge:		
5. Commitment to face challenge:		
6. Feeling out challenge:		
7. Preparing for ultimate challenge:		
8. First attempt:		
9. Results of first attempt:		
10. Second acknowledgment of challenge:		
11. Face final challenge:		
12. Defeating final challenge:		

CHARACTER ARC WORKSHEET

Screenplay/Project: _____ Date: _____

ACT 1	ACT 2	ACT 3

Character Name: _____ ☐ Main ☐ Supporting

	PHYSICAL	EMOTIONAL
1. Normal life (without challenge):		
2. Introduced to challenge:		
3. Denial of challenge:		
4. First acknowledgment of challenge:		
5. Commitment to face challenge:		
6. Feeling out challenge:		
7. Preparing for ultimate challenge:		
8. First attempt:		
9. Results of first attempt:		
10. Second acknowledgment of challenge:		
11. Face final challenge:		
12. Defeating final challenge:		

John has learned two things:
1. He has butterfingers.
2. Organizing story lines on index cards
isn't the greatest idea.

Chapter 8

PLOT CHART

Now that you've finished the Plot Structure, Plot Points and Character Arc worksheets, it's time to combine them and see what your finished story blueprints look like. In the Plot Chart we have combined plot points, plot structure and character arc, overlapping them where necessary so you, the writer, can see the whole picture.

Plot Points + Plot Structure + Character Arc = Plot Chart

We've covered all these topics, but it's not always easy to visualize how they can be combined. Which elements can overlap? What page numbers are shared by separate elements? How the heck are you supposed to organize all the information you've compiled about your story? The plot chart answers these questions in a way never attempted before.

This finished worksheet is an excellent tool to create an outline, write a synopsis, or even pitch a screenplay. If you can fill out this form from beginning to end, excellent, you know your story! If you can't, look back at your Plot Points, Plot Structure and Character Arc worksheets.

The Plot Chart worksheet is great for finding gaps between the layers of plot and character. If your story is seamless, great—so start writing it, already!

If you find gaps, even better, you just saved yourself spending three months writing a script that would need a major overhaul the minute you arrived at The End.

JEREMY'S INSIDE SCOOP

When you write your script and prepare to send it out, pretend your mother is standing over your shoulder, making sure every nook and cranny of your room (script) is vacuumed, dusted and tidied up. Better yet, pretend your mom is a Navy SEAL drill sergeant. Neatness counts! I've read scripts with coffee stains on the covers, crooked photocopied pages, blank pages in the middle of nowhere, notes scribbled on margins and unbound pages falling out. It would be easier for you to save your postage money and throw the script in the trash yourself.

Presentation reflects a person's determination, determination reflects a person's passion, and passion reflects the desire to write well. An impeccably neat script is a welcome breath of fresh air—the reader knows this writer can be taken seriously, because the writer has taken his script seriously enough to make sure it's properly dressed. Remember, no one at the annual business gala takes the guy in blue jeans very seriously. Don't be the guy in blue jeans.

EASY TO FOLLOW INSTRUCTIONS...

Using this plot chart is a piece of cake! Simply take key elements from each worksheet and combine them into succinct, powerful sentences that describe your screenplay blow by blow.

You'll notice that page numbers are listed for each section. These are merely guidelines. If you're an experienced and professional writer, you have the liberty and clout to break these rules. You may even be expected to. But if you have yet to sell a screenplay and want to sell a screenplay, try and keep your story elements within these page suggestions. You'll be in good shape if you do.

The sections marked "Details" are for any specifics you might want to remember. If you have an idea of specific scenes, stunning visuals, or key dialogue for any of the categories, mark them here. That's it! Get started and watch your story take shape!

Screenplay/Project: _____   Date: _____

1. EXPOSITION (HOOK) (page 1-5)

DETAILS
_____
_____
_____
_____
_____
_____
_____
_____

2. NORMAL LIFE (RISING ACTION) (page 1-10)

DETAILS
_____
_____
_____
_____
_____
_____
_____
_____

3. INTRODUCED TO CHALLENGE (RISING ACTION) (page 5-15)

DETAILS
_____
_____
_____
_____
_____
_____
_____
_____

4. DENIAL OF CHALLENGE (RISING ACTION) (page 10-20)

DETAILS
_____
_____
_____
_____
_____
_____

Screenplay/Project: _____   Date: _____

5. FIRST ACKNOWLEDGMENT OF CHALLENGE (RISING ACTION) (page 15-25)

DETAILS
_____
_____
_____
_____
_____
_____
_____

6. COMMITMENT TO FACE CHALLENGE (PLOT POINT 1) (page 20-30)

DETAILS
_____
_____
_____
_____
_____
_____
_____

7. FEELING OUT THE CHALLENGE (CONFLICT) (page 25-60)

DETAILS
_____
_____
_____
_____
_____
_____
_____

8. TURNING POINT (page 55-65)

DETAILS
_____
_____
_____
_____

Screenplay/Project: _____   Date: _____

9. PREPARING FOR ULTIMATE CHALLENGE (CONFLICT) (page 60-75)

DETAILS
_____
_____
_____
_____
_____
_____
_____
_____

10. RESULTS OF FIRST ATTEMPT (CLIMAX) (page 75-85)

DETAILS
_____
_____
_____
_____
_____
_____
_____
_____

11. SECOND ACKNOWLEDGMENT OF CHALLENGE (PLOT POINT 2) (page 80-90)

DETAILS
_____
_____
_____
_____
_____
_____
_____
_____

12. FACING THE FINAL CHALLENGE (FALLING ACTION) (page 90-110)

DETAILS
_____
_____
_____
_____
_____
_____

Screenplay/Project: _____ Date: _____

13. DEFEATING FINAL CHALLENGE (RESOLUTION) (page 100-115)

_____

_____

_____

DETAILS _____

_____

_____

_____

_____

14. DENOUEMENT (END) (page 110-120)

_____

_____

_____

DETAILS _____

_____

_____

_____

_____

Screenplay/Project: _____ Date: _____

1. EXPOSITION (HOOK) (page 1-5)

DETAILS _____
_____
_____
_____
_____
_____
_____

2. NORMAL LIFE (RISING ACTION) (page 1-10)

DETAILS _____
_____
_____
_____
_____
_____
_____

3. INTRODUCED TO CHALLENGE (RISING ACTION) (page 5-15)

DETAILS _____
_____
_____
_____
_____
_____
_____

4. DENIAL OF CHALLENGE (RISING ACTION) (page 10-20)

DETAILS _____
_____
_____
_____

Screenplay/Project: _____   Date: _____

5. FIRST ACKNOWLEDGMENT OF CHALLENGE (RISING ACTION) (page 15-25)

_____
_____
_____

DETAILS _____
_____
_____
_____
_____

6. COMMITMENT TO FACE CHALLENGE (PLOT POINT 1) (page 20-30)

_____
_____
_____

DETAILS _____
_____
_____
_____
_____

7. FEELING OUT THE CHALLENGE (CONFLICT) (page 25-60)

_____
_____
_____

DETAILS _____
_____
_____
_____
_____

8. TURNING POINT (page 55-65)

_____
_____
_____

DETAILS _____
_____
_____
_____

PLOT CHART WORKSHEET 3

The Screenplay Workbook

Screenplay/Project: _____ Date: _____

9. PREPARING FOR ULTIMATE CHALLENGE (CONFLICT) (page 60-75)

DETAILS
_____
_____
_____
_____
_____
_____
_____
_____

10. RESULTS OF FIRST ATTEMPT (CLIMAX) (page 75-85)

DETAILS
_____
_____
_____
_____
_____
_____
_____
_____

11. SECOND ACKNOWLEDGMENT OF CHALLENGE (PLOT POINT 2) (page 80-90)

DETAILS
_____
_____
_____
_____
_____
_____
_____
_____

12. FACING THE FINAL CHALLENGE (FALLING ACTION) (page 90-110)

DETAILS
_____
_____
_____
_____
_____
_____

Screenplay/Project: _____ Date: _____

13. DEFEATING FINAL CHALLENGE (RESOLUTION) (page 100-115)

DETAILS

_____

_____

_____

_____

_____

_____

_____

_____

14. DENOUEMENT (END) (page 110-120)

DETAILS

_____

_____

_____

_____

_____

_____

_____

Screenplay/Project: _____ Date: _____

1. EXPOSITION (HOOK) (page 1-5)

_____

_____

_____

DETAILS _____

_____

_____

_____

2. NORMAL LIFE (RISING ACTION) (page 1-10)

_____

_____

_____

DETAILS _____

_____

_____

_____

3. INTRODUCED TO CHALLENGE (RISING ACTION) (page 5-15)

_____

_____

_____

DETAILS _____

_____

_____

_____

4. DENIAL OF CHALLENGE (RISING ACTION) (page 10-20)

_____

_____

_____

DETAILS _____

_____

_____

_____

Screenplay/Project: _____ Date: _____

5. FIRST ACKNOWLEDGMENT OF CHALLENGE (RISING ACTION) (page 15-25)

DETAILS

_____
_____
_____
_____
_____
_____
_____

6. COMMITMENT TO FACE CHALLENGE (PLOT POINT 1) (page 20-30)

DETAILS

_____
_____
_____
_____
_____
_____
_____

7. FEELING OUT THE CHALLENGE (CONFLICT) (page 25-60)

DETAILS

_____
_____
_____
_____
_____
_____
_____

8. TURNING POINT (page 55-65)

DETAILS

_____
_____
_____
_____
_____

Screenplay/Project: _____   Date: _____

9. PREPARING FOR ULTIMATE CHALLENGE (CONFLICT) (page 60-75)

_____
_____
_____

DETAILS _____
_____
_____
_____

10. RESULTS OF FIRST ATTEMPT (CLIMAX) (page 75-85)

_____
_____
_____

DETAILS _____
_____
_____
_____

11. SECOND ACKNOWLEDGMENT OF CHALLENGE (PLOT POINT 2) (page 80-90)

_____
_____
_____

DETAILS _____
_____
_____
_____

12. FACING THE FINAL CHALLENGE (FALLING ACTION) (page 90-110)

_____
_____
_____

DETAILS _____
_____
_____
_____

Screenplay/Project: _____ Date: _____

13. DEFEATING FINAL CHALLENGE (RESOLUTION) (page 100-115)

DETAILS

_____
_____
_____
_____
_____
_____
_____
_____

14. DENOUEMENT (END) (page 110-120)

DETAILS

_____
_____
_____
_____
_____
_____
_____

PLOT CHART WORKSHEET 1

Screenplay/Project: _____ Date: _____

1. EXPOSITION (HOOK) (page 1-5)

_____
_____
_____

DETAILS _____
_____
_____
_____
_____

2. NORMAL LIFE (RISING ACTION) (page 1-10)

_____
_____
_____

DETAILS _____
_____
_____
_____
_____

3. INTRODUCED TO CHALLENGE (RISING ACTION) (page 5-15)

_____
_____
_____

DETAILS _____
_____
_____
_____
_____

4. DENIAL OF CHALLENGE (RISING ACTION) (page 10-20)

_____
_____
_____

DETAILS _____
_____
_____
_____

Screenplay/Project: _____   Date: _____

5. FIRST ACKNOWLEDGMENT OF CHALLENGE (RISING ACTION) (page 15-25)

_____
_____
_____

DETAILS   _____
_____
_____
_____
_____

6. COMMITMENT TO FACE CHALLENGE (PLOT POINT 1) (page 20-30)

_____
_____
_____

DETAILS   _____
_____
_____
_____
_____

7. FEELING OUT THE CHALLENGE (CONFLICT) (page 25-60)

_____
_____
_____

DETAILS   _____
_____
_____
_____
_____

8. TURNING POINT (page 55-65)

_____
_____
_____

DETAILS   _____
_____
_____

Screenplay/Project: _____   Date: _____

9. PREPARING FOR ULTIMATE CHALLENGE (CONFLICT) (page 60-75)

_____
_____
_____

DETAILS
_____
_____
_____
_____
_____

10. RESULTS OF FIRST ATTEMPT (CLIMAX) (page 75-85)

_____
_____
_____

DETAILS
_____
_____
_____
_____
_____

11. SECOND ACKNOWLEDGMENT OF CHALLENGE (PLOT POINT 2) (page 80-90)

_____
_____
_____

DETAILS
_____
_____
_____
_____
_____

12. FACING THE FINAL CHALLENGE (FALLING ACTION) (page 90-110)

_____
_____
_____

DETAILS
_____
_____
_____

Screenplay/Project: _____   Date: _____

13. DEFEATING FINAL CHALLENGE (RESOLUTION) (page 100-115)

_____
_____
_____
DETAILS   _____
_____
_____
_____

14. DENOUEMENT (END) (page 110-120)

_____
_____
_____
DETAILS   _____
_____
_____
_____

Screenplay/Project: _____ Date: _____

1. EXPOSITION (HOOK) (page 1-5)

_____
_____
_____

DETAILS _____
_____
_____
_____

2. NORMAL LIFE (RISING ACTION) (page 1-10)

_____
_____
_____

DETAILS _____
_____
_____
_____

3. INTRODUCED TO CHALLENGE (RISING ACTION) (page 5-15)

_____
_____
_____

DETAILS _____
_____
_____
_____

4. DENIAL OF CHALLENGE (RISING ACTION) (page 10-20)

_____
_____
_____

DETAILS _____
_____
_____

Screenplay/Project: _____   Date: _____

5. FIRST ACKNOWLEDGMENT OF CHALLENGE (RISING ACTION) (page 15-25)

DETAILS
_____
_____
_____
_____
_____
_____
_____
_____
_____

6. COMMITMENT TO FACE CHALLENGE (PLOT POINT 1) (page 20-30)

DETAILS
_____
_____
_____
_____
_____
_____
_____
_____
_____

7. FEELING OUT THE CHALLENGE (CONFLICT) (page 25-60)

DETAILS
_____
_____
_____
_____
_____
_____
_____
_____
_____

8. TURNING POINT (page 55-65)

DETAILS
_____
_____
_____
_____
_____
_____
_____

Screenplay/Project: _____ Date: _____

9. PREPARING FOR ULTIMATE CHALLENGE (CONFLICT) (page 60-75)

_____
_____
_____

DETAILS _____
_____
_____
_____

10. RESULTS OF FIRST ATTEMPT (CLIMAX) (page 75-85)

_____
_____
_____

DETAILS _____
_____
_____
_____

11. SECOND ACKNOWLEDGMENT OF CHALLENGE (PLOT POINT 2) (page 80-90)

_____
_____
_____

DETAILS _____
_____
_____
_____

12. FACING THE FINAL CHALLENGE (FALLING ACTION) (page 90-110)

_____
_____
_____

DETAILS _____
_____
_____
_____

Screenplay/Project: _____   Date: _____

13. DEFEATING FINAL CHALLENGE (RESOLUTION) (page 100-115)

DETAILS

_____
_____
_____
_____
_____
_____
_____

14. DENOUEMENT (END) (page 110-120)

DETAILS

_____
_____
_____
_____
_____
_____
_____

John would soon learn that partaking in a dramatic reading of *Gladiator* with over-zealous method actors was a very big mistake.

Chapter 9

SCENE BY SCENE

The job of a screenwriter is similar to that of a ringside boxing announcer. Concise, powerful statements detail every bone crushing punch. The entire fight, right up to the climax is described, blow-by-blow, so that the entire picture can be experienced, without actually seeing it. Screenwriters must do the same when they write a screenplay.

Screenplays are broken up into chunks of action called scenes. But what defines a scene? Scenes are usually somewhere between one paragraph to three pages long. They may run longer, but not often. They can be filled with dialogue and action, but only one location. As soon as the story moves to a new location or time, it has entered a new scene.

A scene should not to be confused with a sequence, which is composed of several scenes. For instance—a car chase is not a scene. Every new street, bridge and alley starts a new scene. Every time the point of view changes from inside the car to outside the car begins a new scene.

Scenes are the building blocks of screenplays. Look at scenes like a pile of Lego blocks. Assemble them one way, you get a space ship. Rearrange them and you have a submarine. Rearrange them without care one more time and you have a pile of Lego blocks. The way your scenes are put together determines how much of an impact your screenplay deals out. One formation gets you a space adventure; another may result in a cleanup job that leaves you grounded without TV privileges.

But what makes up the internal structure of a scene? They have to be more complex than a Lego piece, right? Just like a screenplay, every scene is like a miniature story. Each has a beginning, climax and ending. A scene can be laid out with a compressed story structure including rising action, climax and falling action. Scenes begin with action leading towards an objective; new elements are introduced and the scene exits headed in a new direction.

EXAMPLE: Fred is determined to break up with his girlfriend, Rachel. He enters the living room to find her scantily clad on the couch. Fred, against his better judgement finds her irresistible, the two fall onto the couch—steamy lovemaking ensues.

Fred entered the living room as the scene began. He sees his girlfriend looking sexy on the couch and the action takes an unexpected twist. Fred becomes aroused and falls prey to his soon-to-be ex-girlfriend. This scene pulls you in by Fred's determination. It twists things around by having Fred fool around with the girl he's breaking up with and then leaves things in a worse state then they were when the scene began, pushing the story forward and pulling an eager audience into the next scene.

There are two types of scenes in a screenplay: Major and Minor. Minor scenes are very short scenes in which very few lines of dialogue, if any, are exchanged. They can be a shot of a city skyline, a car driving past or quick shot during an action sequence. This type of scene functions as glue. Minor scenes meld your major scenes together and hold them in place.

Major scenes are the meat of your screenplay. Each is like a juicy chunk of steak that should leave the audience wanting another piece. Each scene pulls the audience deeper and deeper into the story, twisting the characters in new directions. Major scenes are blocks of action and dialogue that take place in one place and move the story forward. Each major scene has key dialogue, key action and a revelation that further enthralls the audience.

EXAMPLE: Fred walks to and opens the living room door (minor scene).

- Fred is determined to break up with his girlfriend, Rachel. He enters the living room to find her scantily clad on the couch. Fred, against his better judgement finds her irresistible, the two fall onto the couch—steamy lovemaking ensues (major scene).
- Time has passed. Rachel can be heard showering in the bathroom. Fred, in the kitchen, takes a shot of whiskey (minor scene).
- Fred re-enters the living room with a determined look on his face. He walks through the living room and into the bedroom (minor scene).
- Fred walks through the bedroom and enters the bathroom (minor scene).
- Fred enters the bathroom, but before he can say anything, Rachel peeks her smiling face out of the curtain and says, "I love you." Fred stumbles over his words as he attempts to end the relationship before things get more complicated. But before Fred can recover, Rachel adds, "Oh, I forgot to tell you. I went off my birth control pills two months ago. I probably should have mentioned that earlier, huh?" Fred's eyes bulge and he runs out of the bathroom (major scene).

It's very helpful to have major scenes worked out in advance. Use the Scene By Scene Worksheet to construct every major scene in your story. Arrange and rearrange them as needed until you have the perfect blow-by-blow layout for your story. When you sit down to write your screenplay you'll find yourself writing steadily, filling in the minor scene glue and conserving creative energy needed to make every major scene an uppercut.

JEREMY'S INSIDE SCOOP

Moving to Los Angeles. This is a sore subject for many a screenwriter. Should you move to Los Angeles? What about the smog, riots, forest fires, mudslides, earthquakes and gangs? Well, it's true, all those things exist in Los Angeles, but with some careful selection it is possible to find a very nice and safe place to live. But you're not moving to Los Angeles for a nice place to live, you're moving to further your career.

If you want to write for TV, move and plan on staying. If you want to write feature films, move, establish yourself as a writer, make contacts, get an agent or manager and then feel free to live wherever you want. It's more important that you're pumping out masterpieces than it is for you to have an Los Angeles address. After you get an agent or manager, that address is the only one people will see.

But will moving to Los Angeles really help? Yes. I have done more in my two years in Los Angeles then in my previous five on the East Coast. You'll make connections, learn the trade quickly and make connections. Did I say connections twice? It's worth repeating. It's worth committing to memory. Hollywood isn't always about how well you write, it's often about who you know. Really.

EASY TO FOLLOW INSTRUCTIONS...

STEP 1: DETAILS
Choose the act in which you want your scene to take place. Number the scenes in the order you think they'll appear in your script.

STEP 2: WHERE AND WHEN
Choose the time and place your scene occurs. EXT. stands for exterior (outside), INT. stands for interior (inside).

STEP 3: TYPE OF SCENE
Here you can choose to identify your scene with a specific plot point or story structure element. This helps you keep the scene on track, heading toward a specific goal.

STEP 4: CHARACTERS PRESENT

List all characters who appear in the scene, even if they don't have dialogue. If you have a large group of people simply refer to them as "crowd of people," or something more appropriate to your situation.

STEP 5: VISUAL DESCRIPTION

This is where you describe the scenery. Does the scene take place inside a bowling ally? A restaurant? What kind? What does it look like? Does the scene take place on top of a mountain? Is there a sunset? Write down all significant visual details.

STEP 6: KEY ACTION

Write down every major action that takes place in this scene. Does a car crash? Is someone shot? Is someone caught picking his nose? What action stands out in this scene?

STEP 7: KEY DIALOGUE

Write down any dialogue for this scene that's already standing out in your mind. This could be a catch phrase such as, "I'll be back," or simply a reminder to yourself as to what the general conversation should entail.

STEP 8: REVELATION OF SCENE

Every scene moves the story forward through revelation. The audience and your characters know something they didn't when the scene began. What is it? What fact will make the audience watch the next scene?

STEP 9: SCENE SUMMARY

Give a brief synopsis of the entire story arc for this scene. Start at the beginning, include the climax and describe how the scene ends. Bring together all previous steps in an easily understood two or three sentence paragraph.

The Screenplay Workbook

SCENE WORKSHEET

Screenplay/Project: _____ Date: _____

☐ Act 1 ☐ Act 2 ☐ Act 3 Scene Number: _____

☐ AM ☐ EXT.
Time: _____ ☐ PM Place: _____ ☐ INT.

TYPE OF SCENE

☐ Plot Point 1 ☐ Turning Point ☐ Climax ☐ Other: _____
☐ Plot Point 2 ☐ Rising Action ☐ Falling Action _____

CHARACTERS PRESENT

_____ _____ _____
_____ _____ _____
_____ _____ _____
_____ _____ _____

VISUAL DESCRIPTION

_____
_____

KEY ACTION

_____
_____

KEY DIALOGUE

_____
_____
_____

REVELATION OF SCENE

_____

SCENE SUMMARY

_____
_____
_____

The Screenplay Workbook

SCENE WORKSHEET

Screenplay/Project: _____ Date: _____

☐ Act 1   ☐ Act 2   ☐ Act 3   Scene Number: _____

☐ AM   ☐ EXT.
Time: _____ ☐ PM   Place: _____   ☐ INT.

TYPE OF SCENE

☐ Plot Point 1   ☐ Turning Point   ☐ Climax   ☐ Other: _____
☐ Plot Point 2   ☐ Rising Action   ☐ Falling Action   _____

CHARACTERS PRESENT

_____   _____   _____
_____   _____   _____
_____   _____   _____
_____   _____   _____

VISUAL DESCRIPTION

_____
_____

KEY ACTION

_____
_____

KEY DIALOGUE

_____
_____
_____

REVELATION OF SCENE

_____

SCENE SUMMARY

_____
_____
_____

SCENE WORKSHEET

Screenplay/Project: _____   Date: _____

☐ Act 1   ☐ Act 2   ☐ Act 3   Scene Number: _____

☐ AM
Time: _____ ☐ PM   Place: _____   ☐ EXT.
                                                          ☐ INT.

TYPE OF SCENE

☐ Plot Point 1   ☐ Turning Point   ☐ Climax   ☐ Other: _____
☐ Plot Point 2   ☐ Rising Action   ☐ Falling Action _____

CHARACTERS PRESENT

_____   _____   _____
_____   _____   _____
_____   _____   _____
_____   _____   _____

VISUAL DESCRIPTION

_____
_____

KEY ACTION

_____
_____

KEY DIALOGUE

_____
_____
_____

REVELATION OF SCENE

_____

SCENE SUMMARY

_____
_____
_____

SCENE WORKSHEET

Screenplay/Project: _____ Date: _____

☐ Act 1   ☐ Act 2   ☐ Act 3   Scene Number: _____

Time: _____   ☐ AM   Place: _____   ☐ EXT.
                 ☐ PM   ☐ INT.

TYPE OF SCENE

☐ Plot Point 1   ☐ Turning Point   ☐ Climax   ☐ Other: _____
☐ Plot Point 2   ☐ Rising Action   ☐ Falling Action   _____

CHARACTERS PRESENT

_____   _____   _____
_____   _____   _____
_____   _____   _____
_____   _____   _____

VISUAL DESCRIPTION

_____
_____

KEY ACTION

_____
_____

KEY DIALOGUE

_____
_____
_____

REVELATION OF SCENE

_____

SCENE SUMMARY

_____
_____
_____

SCENE WORKSHEET

Screenplay/Project: _____ **Date:** _____

☐ Act 1   ☐ Act 2   ☐ Act 3   Scene Number: _____

☐ AM
Time: _____ ☐ PM   **Place:** _____   ☐ EXT.
                                                              ☐ INT.

TYPE OF SCENE

☐ Plot Point 1   ☐ Turning Point   ☐ Climax   ☐ Other: _____
☐ Plot Point 2   ☐ Rising Action   ☐ Falling Action   _____

CHARACTERS PRESENT

_____   _____   _____
_____   _____   _____
_____   _____   _____
_____   _____   _____

VISUAL DESCRIPTION

_____
_____

KEY ACTION

_____
_____

KEY DIALOGUE

_____
_____
_____

REVELATION OF SCENE

_____

SCENE SUMMARY

_____
_____
_____

SCENE WORKSHEET

Screenplay/Project: _____ Date: _____

☐ Act 1   ☐ Act 2   ☐ Act 3   Scene Number: _____

☐ AM   ☐ EXT.
Time: _____ ☐ PM   Place: _____ ☐ INT.

TYPE OF SCENE

☐ Plot Point 1   ☐ Turning Point   ☐ Climax   ☐ Other: _____
☐ Plot Point 2   ☐ Rising Action   ☐ Falling Action   _____

CHARACTERS PRESENT

_____   _____   _____

_____   _____   _____

_____   _____   _____

_____   _____   _____

VISUAL DESCRIPTION

_____

_____

KEY ACTION

_____

_____

KEY DIALOGUE

_____

_____

_____

REVELATION OF SCENE

_____

SCENE SUMMARY

_____

_____

_____

SCENE WORKSHEET

Screenplay/Project: _____ Date: _____

☐ Act 1   ☐ Act 2   ☐ Act 3   Scene Number: _____

Time: _____ ☐ AM
              ☐ PM   Place: _____   ☐ EXT.
                                                        ☐ INT.

TYPE OF SCENE

☐ Plot Point 1   ☐ Turning Point   ☐ Climax   ☐ Other: _____
☐ Plot Point 2   ☐ Rising Action   ☐ Falling Action _____

CHARACTERS PRESENT

_____   _____   _____
_____   _____   _____
_____   _____   _____
_____   _____   _____

VISUAL DESCRIPTION

_____
_____

KEY ACTION

_____
_____

KEY DIALOGUE

_____
_____
_____

REVELATION OF SCENE

_____

SCENE SUMMARY

_____
_____
_____

Screenplay/Project: _____   Date: _____

☐ Act 1   ☐ Act 2   ☐ Act 3   Scene Number: _____

☐ AM   ☐ EXT.
Time: _____   ☐ PM   Place: _____   ☐ INT.

TYPE OF SCENE

☐ Plot Point 1   ☐ Turning Point   ☐ Climax   ☐ Other: _____
☐ Plot Point 2   ☐ Rising Action   ☐ Falling Action
                                                            _____

CHARACTERS PRESENT

_____   _____   _____

_____   _____   _____

_____   _____   _____

_____   _____   _____

VISUAL DESCRIPTION

_____

_____

KEY ACTION

_____

_____

KEY DIALOGUE

_____

_____

_____

REVELATION OF SCENE

_____

SCENE SUMMARY

_____

_____

_____

Screenplay/Project: _____   Date: _____

☐ Act 1   ☐ Act 2   ☐ Act 3   Scene Number: _____

☐ AM   ☐ EXT.
Time: _____   ☐ PM   Place: _____   ☐ INT.

TYPE OF SCENE

☐ Plot Point 1   ☐ Turning Point   ☐ Climax   ☐ Other: _____
☐ Plot Point 2   ☐ Rising Action   ☐ Falling Action   _____

CHARACTERS PRESENT

_____   _____   _____
_____   _____   _____
_____   _____   _____
_____   _____   _____

VISUAL DESCRIPTION

_____
_____

KEY ACTION

_____
_____

KEY DIALOGUE

_____
_____
_____

REVELATION OF SCENE

_____

SCENE SUMMARY

_____
_____
_____

Screenplay/Project: _____ Date: _____

☐ Act 1   ☐ Act 2   ☐ Act 3   Scene Number: _____

Time: _____   ☐ AM   ☐ PM   Place: _____   ☐ EXT.   ☐ INT.

TYPE OF SCENE

☐ Plot Point 1   ☐ Turning Point   ☐ Climax   ☐ Other: _____
☐ Plot Point 2   ☐ Rising Action   ☐ Falling Action   _____

CHARACTERS PRESENT

_____   _____   _____
_____   _____   _____
_____   _____   _____
_____   _____   _____

VISUAL DESCRIPTION

_____
_____

KEY ACTION

_____
_____

KEY DIALOGUE

_____
_____
_____

REVELATION OF SCENE

_____

SCENE SUMMARY

_____
_____

SCENE WORKSHEET

Screenplay/Project: _____   Date: _____

☐ Act 1   ☐ Act 2   ☐ Act 3   Scene Number: _____

Time: _____   ☐ AM   Place: _____   ☐ EXT.
                  ☐ PM   ☐ INT.

TYPE OF SCENE

☐ Plot Point 1   ☐ Turning Point   ☐ Climax   ☐ Other: _____
☐ Plot Point 2   ☐ Rising Action   ☐ Falling Action   _____

CHARACTERS PRESENT

_____   _____   _____
_____   _____   _____
_____   _____   _____
_____   _____   _____

VISUAL DESCRIPTION

_____
_____

KEY ACTION

_____
_____

KEY DIALOGUE

_____
_____
_____

REVELATION OF SCENE

_____

SCENE SUMMARY

_____
_____
_____

The Screenplay Workbook

SCENE WORKSHEET

Screenplay/Project: _____ Date: _____

☐ Act 1 ☐ Act 2 ☐ Act 3 Scene Number: _____

☐ AM   ☐ EXT.
Time: _____ ☐ PM   Place: _____   ☐ INT.

TYPE OF SCENE

☐ Plot Point 1   ☐ Turning Point   ☐ Climax   ☐ Other: _____
☐ Plot Point 2   ☐ Rising Action   ☐ Falling Action _____

CHARACTERS PRESENT

_____   _____   _____
_____   _____   _____
_____   _____   _____
_____   _____   _____

VISUAL DESCRIPTION

_____
_____

KEY ACTION

_____
_____

KEY DIALOGUE

_____
_____
_____

REVELATION OF SCENE

_____

SCENE SUMMARY

_____
_____

SCENE WORKSHEET

Screenplay/Project: _____ Date: _____

☐ Act 1   ☐ Act 2   ☐ Act 3   Scene Number: _____

Time: _____   ☐ AM   Place: _____   ☐ EXT.
                  ☐ PM   ☐ INT.

TYPE OF SCENE

☐ Plot Point 1   ☐ Turning Point   ☐ Climax   ☐ Other: _____
☐ Plot Point 2   ☐ Rising Action   ☐ Falling Action _____

CHARACTERS PRESENT

_____   _____   _____
_____   _____   _____
_____   _____   _____
_____   _____   _____

VISUAL DESCRIPTION

_____
_____

KEY ACTION

_____
_____

KEY DIALOGUE

_____
_____
_____

REVELATION OF SCENE

_____

SCENE SUMMARY

_____
_____

Screenplay/Project: _____   Date: _____

☐ Act 1   ☐ Act 2   ☐ Act 3   Scene Number: _____

☐ AM   ☐ EXT.
Time: _____ ☐ PM   Place: _____   ☐ INT.

TYPE OF SCENE

☐ Plot Point 1   ☐ Turning Point   ☐ Climax   ☐ Other: _____
☐ Plot Point 2   ☐ Rising Action   ☐ Falling Action   _____

CHARACTERS PRESENT

_____   _____   _____
_____   _____   _____
_____   _____   _____
_____   _____   _____

VISUAL DESCRIPTION

_____
_____

KEY ACTION

_____
_____

KEY DIALOGUE

_____
_____
_____

REVELATION OF SCENE

_____

SCENE SUMMARY

_____
_____

SCENE WORKSHEET

Screenplay/Project: _____   Date: _____

☐ Act 1   ☐ Act 2   ☐ Act 3   Scene Number: _____

                    ☐ AM   ☐ EXT.
Time: _____   ☐ PM   Place: _____   ☐ INT.

TYPE OF SCENE
☐ Plot Point 1   ☐ Turning Point   ☐ Climax   ☐ Other: _____
☐ Plot Point 2   ☐ Rising Action   ☐ Falling Action   _____

CHARACTERS PRESENT

_____   _____   _____
_____   _____   _____
_____   _____   _____
_____   _____   _____

VISUAL DESCRIPTION

_____
_____

KEY ACTION

_____
_____

KEY DIALOGUE

_____
_____
_____

REVELATION OF SCENE

_____

SCENE SUMMARY

_____
_____
_____

SCENE WORKSHEET

Screenplay/Project: _____   Date: _____

☐ Act 1   ☐ Act 2   ☐ Act 3   Scene Number: _____

☐ AM   ☐ EXT.
Time: _____ ☐ PM   Place: _____ ☐ INT.

TYPE OF SCENE

☐ Plot Point 1   ☐ Turning Point   ☐ Climax   ☐ Other: _____
☐ Plot Point 2   ☐ Rising Action   ☐ Falling Action   _____

CHARACTERS PRESENT

_____   _____   _____
_____   _____   _____
_____   _____   _____
_____   _____   _____

VISUAL DESCRIPTION

_____
_____

KEY ACTION

_____
_____

KEY DIALOGUE

_____
_____
_____

REVELATION OF SCENE

_____

SCENE SUMMARY

_____
_____

SCENE WORKSHEET

Screenplay/Project: _____ Date: _____

☐ Act 1   ☐ Act 2   ☐ Act 3   Scene Number: _____

☐ AM   ☐ EXT.
Time: _____ ☐ PM   Place: _____ ☐ INT.

TYPE OF SCENE

☐ Plot Point 1   ☐ Turning Point   ☐ Climax   ☐ Other: _____
☐ Plot Point 2   ☐ Rising Action   ☐ Falling Action _____

CHARACTERS PRESENT

_____   _____   _____
_____   _____   _____
_____   _____   _____
_____   _____   _____

VISUAL DESCRIPTION

_____
_____

KEY ACTION

_____
_____

KEY DIALOGUE

_____
_____
_____

REVELATION OF SCENE

_____

SCENE SUMMARY

_____
_____
_____

SCENE WORKSHEET

Screenplay/Project: _____   Date: _____

- [ ] Act 1   - [ ] Act 2   - [ ] Act 3   Scene Number: _____

Time: _____   - [ ] AM   - [ ] PM   Place: _____   - [ ] EXT.   - [ ] INT.

TYPE OF SCENE

- [ ] Plot Point 1   - [ ] Turning Point   - [ ] Climax   - [ ] Other: _____
- [ ] Plot Point 2   - [ ] Rising Action   - [ ] Falling Action _____

CHARACTERS PRESENT

_____   _____   _____
_____   _____   _____
_____   _____   _____
_____   _____   _____

VISUAL DESCRIPTION

_____
_____

KEY ACTION

_____
_____

KEY DIALOGUE

_____
_____
_____

REVELATION OF SCENE

_____

SCENE SUMMARY

_____
_____
_____

SCENE WORKSHEET

Screenplay/Project: _____ Date: _____

☐ Act 1   ☐ Act 2   ☐ Act 3   Scene Number: _____

☐ AM   ☐ EXT.
Time: _____ ☐ PM   Place: _____   ☐ INT.

TYPE OF SCENE

☐ Plot Point 1   ☐ Turning Point   ☐ Climax   ☐ Other: _____
☐ Plot Point 2   ☐ Rising Action   ☐ Falling Action _____

CHARACTERS PRESENT

_____   _____   _____
_____   _____   _____
_____   _____   _____
_____   _____   _____

VISUAL DESCRIPTION

_____
_____

KEY ACTION

_____
_____

KEY DIALOGUE

_____
_____
_____

REVELATION OF SCENE

_____

SCENE SUMMARY

_____
_____
_____

SCENE WORKSHEET

Screenplay/Project: _____   Date: _____

☐ Act 1   ☐ Act 2   ☐ Act 3   Scene Number: _____

Time: _____   ☐ AM   Place: _____   ☐ EXT.
                  ☐ PM   ☐ INT.

TYPE OF SCENE

☐ Plot Point 1   ☐ Turning Point   ☐ Climax   ☐ Other: _____
☐ Plot Point 2   ☐ Rising Action   ☐ Falling Action   _____

CHARACTERS PRESENT

_____   _____   _____
_____   _____   _____
_____   _____   _____
_____   _____   _____

VISUAL DESCRIPTION

_____
_____

KEY ACTION

_____
_____

KEY DIALOGUE

_____
_____
_____

REVELATION OF SCENE

_____

SCENE SUMMARY

_____
_____

SCENE WORKSHEET

Screenplay/Project: _____   Date:_____

☐ Act 1   ☐ Act 2   ☐ Act 3   Scene Number:_____

Time: _____   ☐ AM   Place: _____   ☐ EXT.
                  ☐ PM   ☐ INT.

TYPE OF SCENE

☐ Plot Point 1   ☐ Turning Point   ☐ Climax   ☐ Other: _____
☐ Plot Point 2   ☐ Rising Action   ☐ Falling Action _____

CHARACTERS PRESENT

_____   _____   _____
_____   _____   _____
_____   _____   _____
_____   _____   _____

VISUAL DESCRIPTION

_____
_____

KEY ACTION

_____
_____

KEY DIALOGUE

_____
_____
_____

REVELATION OF SCENE

_____

SCENE SUMMARY

_____
_____
_____

SCENE WORKSHEET

Screenplay/Project: _____   Date: _____

☐ Act 1   ☐ Act 2   ☐ Act 3   Scene Number: _____

Time: _____   ☐ AM   Place: _____   ☐ EXT.
               ☐ PM   ☐ INT.

TYPE OF SCENE

☐ Plot Point 1   ☐ Turning Point   ☐ Climax   ☐ Other: _____
☐ Plot Point 2   ☐ Rising Action   ☐ Falling Action _____

CHARACTERS PRESENT

_____   _____   _____
_____   _____   _____
_____   _____   _____
_____   _____   _____

VISUAL DESCRIPTION

_____
_____

KEY ACTION

_____
_____

KEY DIALOGUE

_____
_____
_____

REVELATION OF SCENE

_____

SCENE SUMMARY

_____
_____
_____

SCENE WORKSHEET

Screenplay/Project: _____   Date: _____

☐ Act 1   ☐ Act 2   ☐ Act 3   Scene Number: _____

☐ AM   ☐ EXT.
Time: _____ ☐ PM   Place: _____   ☐ INT.

TYPE OF SCENE

☐ Plot Point 1   ☐ Turning Point   ☐ Climax   ☐ Other: _____
☐ Plot Point 2   ☐ Rising Action   ☐ Falling Action   _____

CHARACTERS PRESENT

_____   _____   _____
_____   _____   _____
_____   _____   _____
_____   _____   _____

VISUAL DESCRIPTION

_____
_____

KEY ACTION

_____
_____

KEY DIALOGUE

_____
_____
_____

REVELATION OF SCENE

_____

SCENE SUMMARY

_____
_____
_____

WHAT COMES NEXT?

Okay, so you've filled out every worksheet. That's great—you've got your story! You know more about your character's life than you do about your Uncle Phil. Your screenplay has a blueprint with which you can tell your story. But now what?

The writing before the writing is complete; now begins the actual writing. This is the part where you type FADE IN:, hit ENTER twice and then type INT: blah blah blah. But this time you won't see a blank page with so many possibilities that you just stare at it blankly, eyes listless and drool stringing from your slack jaw. This time you have direction and a path to follow. This is the exciting part when you take those worksheets you filled out and put them to good and exciting use.

If, however, you have never written a screenplay before, you have some more prep work to do before you can type the illustrious FADE IN:. Of course, you could go right ahead and start writing (some people learn best from their own mistakes) but we would suggest this as the next logical step: *learn screenplay formatting*. We can't stress this enough. If you write a screenplay like a novel, or even a play, you're wasting your time. Unless you're writing for fun, you're just putting off your future success that much longer.

So how does one learn screenplay format? It's actually not too hard to do, which is why people with poor format get rejected. If you can't take the time to learn something so easy, why should we believe you took the time to learn how to write? The absolute best way to go about assuring your format is kosher is to get screenwriting software. I recommend Final Draft. If you can't afford Final Draft, go on the Web and look for free Word plug-ins or tutorials on how to format. These methods aren't as reliable, but are better than nothing. Check out the resources section at the back of the book for other helpful links.

Lastly, if screenwriting is something you want to do for a career, listen and listen carefully...or, more accurately, *read* carefully: *write every day*. It's probably the most clichéd advice a writer can give, but take a look at who gives that advice—every successful writer in the known universe. There's a reason for it. Writing is extremely competitive. There are more writers in the world then there are jobs for writers. When a runner wants to run a marathon, what do they do? They run every day, even if it's just a mile or two.

The only way to get better at something is to do it often.

That's the best advice we can give. So get started! What are you waiting for? Stop reading this and go fill out some worksheets and write a screenplay!

Good luck!

—Jeremy and Tom

Hey, while you're at it, why don't you drop us a line, we'd like to hear from you! Let us know how the worksheets have worked for you and feel free to suggest future worksheets. We might just add your ideas to a second edition! Jeremy can be reached at: info@offcameraproductions.com. Tom can be reached at: info@vanmungo.com.

Appendix

ONLINE RESOURCES

ABSOLUTE WRITE

"Absolute Write is a popular Web site for writers; covering screenwriting, freelance writing, novels, non-fiction writing and more. The weekly newsletters contain articles; interviews with writers, agents, and producers; humor; and markets and contests for writers. Get free advice from a top screenwriter and a free e-book when you subscribe." This is an all around good resource site for screenwriters and non-screenwriters alike. It also features fun writing jokes and humor columns that are always good for a laugh.
http://www.absolutewrite.com

BABYNAMES.COM

Need help coming up with a name for your new character? Here's the place to do it. You can search by name, meaning of name, names starting with and names ending with. The list of names here is truly expansive. Worth checking out for fun, even if you are a name creating genius.
www.babynames.com

BARTLEBY PROJECT

"The preeminent Internet publisher of literature, reference, and verse providing students, researchers, and the intellectually curious with unlimited access to books and information on the Web, free of charge!" Holy research, Batman! What a wonderful Web site. I mean, you can access the entirety of William Strunk's *The Elements of Style*, the King James version of the Bible, Henry Gray's *Anatomy of the Human Body* and all of

Shakespeare's plays! And there is so much more! This Web site is truly exciting to the literary minded. Best of all, it is 100 percent free!
www.bartleby.com

CLICHÉ FINDER
"Have you been searching for just the right cliché to use? Are you searching for a cliché using the word "cat" or "day" but haven't been able to come up with one? This site will help solve those problems." Whether you want to use a cliché or avoid using one, this is the perfect resource for both. Of course, to you this site might not be anything to write home about. Aha! You see that? That's the Cliché Finder in action.
www.westegg.com/cliche

CREATIVE SCREENWRITING MAGAZINE
"The Web site features discussion groups, classifieds, back issues, subscription information, and an array of articles and interviews, sure to educate and inform screenwriters. One of the few magazines screenwriters should make sure to read every month." Can't say it better then that. You're a screenwriter; you should be reading most screenwriting magazines! If you're broke, as are many screenwriters, just go to the bookstore, get a coffee and read it there. Then again, if you can afford to pay for fancy bookstore coffee, you can afford to buy a magazine!
http://www.creativescreenwriting.com

CRIME LIBRARY
Find thousands of in-depth stories and news on the most notorious crimes of all time. These are very interesting and chilling stories of real-life crimes. This record of detestable acts may chill you, but it makes great material for thriller, horror, and crime screenplays.
www.crimelibrary.com

DICTIONARY.COM
If you don't have a dictionary and thesaurus already and are too poor to buy them, this is an excellent alternative. In truth, this Web site may be superior to the hard copies. Keep the Web site open while you write, switch to dictionary.com whenever you feel the need, type in your query and presto, you have a myriad of words at your fingertips. This site is a bona fide time saver.
www.dictionary.com

DONE DEAL
"Daily news resource for screenplay, pitch, treatment, and books sales in Hollywood, along with interviews with industry professionals, screenwriting software & book reviews, advice, agency, law firms & production company listings, contests, columns, message board & chat room, examples of contracts, script pages, and more." Done Deal is an old favorite. Their industry sales listings are always worth checking out. While this site may not be the prettiest, it's easy to navigate and always useful.
http://www.scriptsales.com

DREW'S SCRIPT-O-RAMA
This Web site hosts loads of screenplays for your downloading enjoyment. Categories include: anime, film scripts, film transcripts, TV scripts, unproduced scripts, movie haikus and contest links. This is a great resource for getting your hands on free scripts. But make sure not to base your formatting on the scripts here: most are incorrect as they have been modified for the Web. Drew's Script-O-Rama is now available is two versions: the old version (easier to navigate in my opinion) and the new jazzed up version, which is pretty, but not quite as functional.
http://www.script-o-rama.com

E-SCRIPT

"E-script, the Internet's scriptwriting workshop, offers online, individualized courses and workshops in screen and television writing. Registrants work one-on-one with professional writers and story editors. In E-script's courses, writers receive weekly tutorials and exercises, intended to get them started on a script; in the workshops, writers work on a draft of a screenplay or television project of their choice. In both, they receive ongoing, personal professional guidance and feedback." I can't personally vouch for this Web site or for online courses in general because I've experienced neither. But if online classes float your boat and you don't have the drive to self-teach using info from the Web or the bazillions of how-to screenwriting books, this might be just the thing you're looking for.

http://www.singlelane.com/escript

FADE IN: MAGAZINE

The online edition of *Fade In* magazine is worth perusing if you like the paper *Fade In* magazine, but lack the funds to purchase it. This site displays interviews, on-location articles and two feature articles straight from the magazine. There is one pop-up ad—it's bearable at first, but quickly becomes annoying after continued browsing.

http://www.fadeinmag.com

FILM THREAT

"Film Threat's mission is to champion the increasingly popular explosion of independent and underground films. For over a decade Film Threat has covered cult films, underground shorts, alternative films and independent features. The magazine was retired in 1997 but lives on in cyberspace." This site is well designed and packed tight with vast amounts of information on every subject imaginable...OK, so maybe you won't find anything on curing toe fungus, but is that really a bad thing? If you're an indie or underground film fan, check this site out. You won't be disappointed.

http://www.filmthreat.com

HARVEST MOON PUBLISHING

"Established in 1992, Harvest Moon Publishing's goal is to establish a growing commercial library of film screenplays and television scripts and to gain these works recognition as legitimate literary forms." If you want to buy professionally published copies of screenplays or teleplays, this is the place to go. However, you can download many scripts from the Internet, print and bind them yourself for far less money—giving you the extra cash to purchase more junk food, thus fueling your next screenplay and accelerating your budding screenwriting career! But if you like having the real deal, this is where to get it.

www.harvestmoon.com

HOLLYWOOD CREATIVE DIRECTORY

If you need to contact someone in Hollywood, but don't have their contact information, have no fear, the Hollywood Creative Directory is here! Find nearly anyone worth mentioning in Hollywood in the pages of this book, which you can order from the HCD Web site as well as Lone Eagle Publishing's other books (including *The Screenplay Workbook!*). The HCD Web site also offers a great job board. The nicest feature about the site is the HCD Online Directory, which you need to pay for, but if you're contacting Hollywood big-wigs and want up-to-date info on where they can be reached, there is no better way.

www.hcdonline.com

HOLLYWOOD SCREENPLAY SOFTWARE

More screenwriting software, though this company's Hollywood Screenplay software seems to offer more than just formatting—like features about story development. (But you have *The Screenplay Workbook* now! You

don't need that. Software will just confuse you. And you can buy, like, eight books for the price of software! But that's just our own biased opinion....) Check this software out for yourself by downloading a free trial.
www.ballisticware.com

HOLLYWOOD SCRIPTWRITER
A nice screenwriting magazine with articles on industry news, the craft, and perspective. The content is always great, but there just isn't enough of it. Closer to being a newsletter than an actual magazine. You can read several of the magazine's articles on the Web site and also become a subscriber.
http://www.hollywoodscriptwriter.com

HOW STUFF WORKS
"Millions of people have described HowStuffWorks content as reliable, accurate and entertaining. Originally founded as a Web site for curious people, the award-winning company now offers clear and fascinating content through various media channels to millions of readers every month. Recognized internationally as the leading provider of information on how things work, HowStuffWorks content explains the world from the inside out!" Screenwriters aren't often experts at too much else other than being screenwriters, so we need a place to find out how some stuff works, or it won't be believable in our screenplays. This Web site is a great resource for doing just that. Beware though, plenty of pop-ups here.
www.howstuffworks.com

MOOVEES.COM
Offers a bizarre combination of film and cows, grading the latest movies with bottles of milk instead of stars (with their patented Milk-o-Meter). In addition to concise, no-bull reviews (no-bull, get it? Ha!) they provide previews for upcoming films, as well as entertaining and interactive movie-related games. And, c'mon, who doesn't love a good cow logo?
www.moovees.com

MOVIE BYTES
"Screenwriting Contests and Markets Online. The MovieBytes Web site features a comprehensive database of screenwriting contests and publishes a free email newsletter. MovieBytes also publishes WhosBuyingWhat.com, an online database of recent screenplay sales, MyScreenplays.com, an online submission tracking service, WinningScripts.com, a database of contest-winning screenplays, and WriterBytes.com, a new weblogging service designed specifically for writers." Sounds like these guys have all their bases covered. Sheesh. If you're looking for a contest to enter, this is definitely the place to go, hands down. And egad, they have a very nice Writer's Wanted section where a nice number of production companies are listed, looking for writers.
http://www.moviebytes.com

MOVIEPOET.COM
"This site provides the latest news, reviews, polls, discussions, and more for screenwriters. Home of the only free, five-page screenplay competition on the Internet. The site is updated daily and is a great resource and inspiration for screenwriters around the world." A bold statement, but this site and its five-page screenplay competition are fun. Winning the contest may not gain you the respect of agents or producers, but you can probably impress your mom, and isn't that what all screenwriters aspire to?
http://www.moviepoet.com

MOVING TO HOLLYWOOD

An interesting site about making the big move to Hollywood—how to prepare and what to expect. The layout is about as poor and bland as a Web site can get, but the information is valid, if a little bit of a buzzkill. If you're looking for some inside info on living in L.A. or want to talk someone out of moving to L.A., this is the site for you.

http://www.io.com/~dbrown/index.html

OFF CAMERA PRODUCTIONS

What's wrong with a shameless plug? Off Camera Productions is the homepage for Jeremy Robinson, author of *The Screenplay Workbook*, which you now hold in your hands. The Web page features news on all of Jeremy's latest projects and offers glimpses of his promotional posters, book covers, and loglines.

www.offcameraproductions.com

THE ONLINE COMMUNICATOR: WRITING

There appears to be a lot of information here on writing for film, video, audio and interactive multimedia, but the layout is distracting enough to frustrate and annoy you. However, the true pioneer may find some useful information here.

http://www.online-communicator.com/writing1.html

THE RESEARCH DEPARTMENT

"A professional research service with access to over 7,000 newspaper and magazine sources from around the world. Provides information to journalists, book authors, screenwriters, and television producers as well as helping private parties and general businesses locate the information they need. In 1992, the *Los Angeles Times* magazine called The Research Department 'possibly Hollywood's highest-tech information gatherer' and 'one of Hollywood's best kept secrets.'" While their services may be worthwhile, the Web site isn't exactly a hotbed for budding writers. This is only for seasoned writers with some spare cash to hire big gun researchers.

www.953info.com

SCREENPLAY.COM

"Screenplay.com is the ultimate free Web site destination for creative writers. It provides tons of tools & resources for writing stage plays, teleplays, and of course, screenplays. Owned and operated by Write Brothers, Inc. (formerly Screenplay Systems). Since 1990, over 80 percent of the Academy® and Emmy® Award nominations have gone to productions that used Write Brothers software!" Ignoring the description above, this site appears to be mostly concerned with promoting software. The Web site may be free, but the software they are selling isn't. However, there are some worthwhile links and articles in the resource area.

www.screenplay.com

SCREENWRITER MAGAZINE

Another great magazine for screenwriters with all the articles, interviews, and news you'd expect. The Web site offers scads of articles straight from the pages of their magazine. The layout is nice and surfing the piles of information on this site is a breeze.

www.nyscreenwriter.com

SCREENWRITER'S CYBERIA

"Screenwriters Cyberia is a resource of links for screenwriters. Established in 1998 with fewer than fifty links, the site has grown to well over a thousand and counting. The site is organized into broad categories including screenwriting, agents, the movie biz, competitions, coverage and more. Each area is rich with links to sites around the Internet pertaining to that subject. Screenwriters Cyberia offers a calendar for easily viewing important competition dates. Visitors to the site can even add their own events and notices to the calendar, free of charge." All true, and easy to navigate, too. But keep in mind, this site provides no real content of its own, just links to other Web sites.

http://www.screenwriterscyberia.com

SCREENWRITER'S FORUM

"An index of links to over 300 screenwriting articles sorted by category, including Character Development, Dialogue, Plot/Story, Genre, Script Format, Selling Your Screenplay, Protecting Your Idea, Research/Resources, Interviews and more, plus monthly columns and book reviews, a forum for unproduced writers, a screenwriting contest, and script consulting services." That says it all. This site truly has a massive collection of how-to articles. Worth a look, especially for new screenwriters.

http://www.screenwritersforum.com

SCREENWRITER'S RESOURCE CENTER

A source for great screenwriting links, software, and more. Compiled by the staff at the National Creative Registry. This being said, Screenwriter's Resource Center is really just a waypoint to other sites. They provide no real content of their own, just links to other Web sites. But if you need a place to start, this might be it.

http://www.screenwriting.com

SCREENWRITER'S UTOPIA

This Web site is well laid out and jam-packed with information, how-to articles, news and interestingly enough—script reviews. Don't see this too often. The reviews are an interesting addition to the common movie review, but are of much greater interest to screenwriters (or at least should be). You can also see script sales at this Web site, though the layout for this particular section isn't as easy to navigate. Worth a look.

http://www.screenwritersutopia.com

SCREENWRITING AT ABOUT.COM

"A highway of information for writers on all levels. The site takes you all the way from that simple idea to the glory of printing out your final draft. With articles on "finding an agent" to "software and book reviews," screenwriting at about.com is a great on-line writing resource." This is a great site with sections like Jobs/Opportunities and Screenwriting 101, but has tons of annoying pop-ups, courtesy of About.com (seriously, if pop-ups annoy you, don't go here without a pop-up stopper).

http://screenwriting.about.com

SCRIPTCRAWLER

A searchable database of downloadable screenplays. Very nice. This is the way every site that provides downloadable screenplays should be presented. However, several links to screenplays are dead. Many screenplays can be found here but finding a link to an elusive screenplay only to click on it and find the page missing...there are few things more frustrating! Brilliant conception and execution, just needs to prune out the dead links.

http://www.scriptcrawler.net

SCR(I)PT MAGAZINE

"The online edition of *scr(i)pt* Magazine. A definitive screenwriting source, scriptmag offers script coverage, proofreading, fact checking, and online screenwriting classes. The *scr(i)pt* Magazine Web site also caters to the Web savvy screenwriter by hosting a page with hundreds of screenwriting links to other proven, useful Web sites that would aid any screenwriter in their pursuit of a perfectly constructed screenplay."

Another must read. Always informative. I hear they have an interesting article about the difference between Science Fiction and Fantasy on this Web site...hmmm, might be worth checking out.
http://www.scriptmag.com

SCRIPT P.I.M.P.

"Script P.I.M.P. is a community based research tool designed for writers and film industry professionals. Since June 2000, Script P.I.M.P. has gathered the specific needs and submission guidelines of production and management companies, literary agencies, independent producers and creative executives searching for new material." This site looks great and sounds great in theory, but you have to be a member to reap the full benefits. If you've got sixty bucks burning a hole in your pocket, go for it, but if you're like most screenwriters, save the money for ink, paper, brads, and food. Plenty of free Web sites offer similar info.
http://www.scriptpimp.com

SCRIPTWARE SOFTWARE

"With Scriptware scriptwriting software you have the fastest, easiest and most powerful way to get the story that's in your head onto the page in the format professionals demand." Well, that's what the Web site says, so it has to be true, right? This software competes with other programs like Final Draft, which is what I use and most of the industry uses, but having never used Scriptware, I can't honestly say which is better. Of course, you can always download the demos for each and decide for yourself.
www.scriptware.com

SCRIPT WRITING SECRETS

This is basically an entire screenwriting how-to book online. *Why* the author would publish the book online and offer it for free to any and all who visit the Web site, I'm not sure. But heck, it's a free screenwriting how-to book! Keep in mind; this book is about how to format a script. An entire book on format! Sheesh, I think we've become obsessed. But seriously, if you need to learn screenplay format and can't afford Final Draft or some other screenwriting software, check out this Web site.
http://www.scriptwritingsecrets.com

SIMPLY SCRIPTS

"The premier resource for scripts, screenplays and transcripts on the net. Read movie scripts, television teleplays, radio transcripts from the Golden Age of Radio, anime scripts and plays. View our showcase of original scripts from some of the hottest writers on the net." Look out Drew! Competition! Many scripts can be found here and the script search engine is a nice touch—I was able to locate scripts incredibly fast—but watch out for pop-up ads, this site is full of them.
http://www.simplyscripts.com

STAR ARCHIVE

"The #1 Guide to Celebrity Addresses. This is a Web site dedicated to helping you to contact your favorite star! On this Web site you can find contact information for thousands of celebrities." It's true; they do have tons of addresses, though not all are accurate. But if you're a stalker or thinking about becoming one, you're in luck! This is the Web site for you.
www.stararchive.com

SUITE101

559 Topics, 26,449 articles, 20,668 links for film/writing resources and 115 online courses. I'd say these guys are going all out. That being said, not everything here is about screenwriting. You'll have to wade through piles of other subjects to find anything on screenwriting. The easiest way to find screenwriting

resources here is to use the search feature and type in "screenwriting." Otherwise, you might be in for a long search.

www.suite101.com

TRANSLATE A FOREIGN LANGUAGE!

Web-based translation service available. And it's free! Translate from English to Spanish, French, German, Portuguese, Italian, etc. Typically Web sites that translate from English to Spanish or any other language translations do it one word at a time. This site goes above and beyond by translating whole sentences, even paragraphs, all at once, up to 10,000 characters! Great for screenplays in which other languages are required. Granted, it's not 100 percent accurate—like a spellcheck, it can only do so much—but it's a great start and very useful.

www.freetranslation.com

WORDS FROM HERE

Oooh, a Flash Web site. "Wordsfromhere.com was set up after the creation of Project Greenlight. It is meant as a meeting place for all kinds of writers." This includes group reviews by peers, links to agencies and production companies as well as writer of the week, movie reviews and site of the week sections. Their "final goal" is "to have a sense of community for writers, coast to coast." Very nice idea. Very nice layout.

http://www.wordsfromhere.com

WRITEMOVIES.COM

This Web site is, as they put it, "A hub for the international film industry receiving millions of hits and affiliated with over 2500 film industry sites world wide!" It is, in fact, available in English, Spanish, Portuguese, French, and Dutch, if you can believe it. First impressions lead the viewer to believe this is simply a screenwriting contest Web site, but a closer look reveals a script consulting service, tons of industry news, and writing tips.

http://www.writemovies.com

THE WRITER AT WORK

"The Writer at Work™ by Richard Krzemien, is a free weekly comic that mixes the working world of DILBERT® with the absurdity of THE FAR SIDE®." These cartoons provide a humorous look at the life of a writer. Small on actual resources but big on laughs, not to mention that Richard is a personable guy. Go Richard!

http://www.thewriteratwork.com

WRITERS GUILD OF AMERICA

If you're a screenwriter—or want to be—and don't know what the Writer's Guild of America is, then go to this Web site *right now*. In fact, even if you are familiar with the Writer's Guild, this is a decent site to visit. Tons of resources from the organization that fights for your rights as a screenwriter. And now you can even register your scripts online! Booyah!

www.wga.org

WRITER'S WRITE: SCREENWRITING

Articles, message boards, classifieds, news and links to production companies. Layout and design is a bit on the dull side, but the content is decent. Most screenwriters should find something useful here. This site is actually a smaller branch of Writer's Write, a Web site that focuses on writing in general. So if you're interested in other forms of writing, simply delete the /screenwriting from the address and voila!

http://www.writerswrite.com/screenwriting